JAZZ BRUSHES
for the Modern Drummer

An Essential Guide to the Art of Keeping Time

by Ulysses Owens Jr.

Book Editor: Megan Rickman

Book Concept Coordinator: Zack Olsen

Cover Art Concept: Chris Horoschak

Cover Art Photo: Miguel Emmanuelli

Illustrations: Taylor Reinhold, Belle Amaral, and Justin Phase

Play-Along Producer: Ulysses Owens Jr. (U.O.J. Productions)

Recording and Mixing Engineers:
Chris Sulit (Trading 8s Studio, Paramus, NJ)
and Dave Darlington (Bass Hit Studios, NYC)

Video Filming, Editing, and Producer: Anna Yatskavich

To access audio and video visit:
www.halleonard.com/mylibrary

Enter Code
7660-0137-6733-7511

ISBN 978-1-5400-5788-4

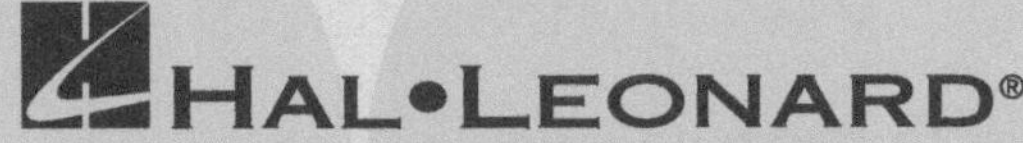

Visit Hal Leonard Online at
www.halleonard.com

Contact us:
Hal Leonard
7777 West Bluemound Road
Milwaukee, WI 53213
Email: info@halleonard.com

In Europe, contact:
Hal Leonard Europe Limited
42 Wigmore Street
Marylebone, London, W1U 2RN
Email: info@halleonardeurope.com

In Australia, contact:
Hal Leonard Australia Pty. Ltd.
4 Lentara Court
Cheltenham, Victoria, 3192 Australia
Email: info@halleonard.com.au

CONTENTS

About the Author

Heralded as a "powerhouse of a showman" (*Glide Magazine*), a "legitimate jazz triple threat" (*Critical Jazz*), and a drummer who "take[s] a back seat to no one" (*The New York Times*), performer, producer, and educator Ulysses Owens Jr. goes to the limit in the jazz world and beyond.

Owens has been named a Rising Star by *DownBeat* magazine's critics' poll for five years straight along with being the third runner-up in the "Classic Jazz Drum" category by *Modern Drummer* magazine's readers' poll. He is a recipient of the 2013 ASCAP Plus Award, the 2014 Global Music Award, and the 2015 Jazz at Lincoln Center Swing! Award.

Owens currently has five albums of his own (*It's Time for U*, *Unanimous*, *Onward and Upward*, *Falling Forward*, and *Songs of Freedom*). He is a Grammy award-winning drummer having gained special attention for his performances on the similarly awarded albums *Dedicated to You* (Kurt Elling) and *The Good Feeling* (Christian McBride Big Band). Owens has also participated on the Grammy award-nominated albums: *Giant Steps* and *Countdown* by Joey Alexander, *Out Here* and *Live at The Village Vanguard* by the Christian McBride Trio, and most recently the album *Nat King Cole & Me* by Gregory Porter.

At the request of Wynton Marsalis and Dr. Aaron Flagg, Owens became an active faculty member of the Jazz Studies Program at his alma mater, the Juilliard School, in 2016. He is a current Visiting Artist in Residence at the Caine College of Arts of Utah State University, and a Faculty Artist in Residence at Edward Waters College in Jacksonville, Florida where he teaches courses in music business.

Ulysses also oversees artistic and community programming for hundreds of children and teens as Artistic Director for Don't Miss a Beat, Inc., a youth-empowerment non-profit organization founded by his family in 2008 in his hometown of Jacksonville, Florida. Education is incredibly important to Ulysses as he seeks to help shape the minds of the next generation of musicians and those that appreciate the performing arts.

Owens's most recent album, *Songs of Freedom*, features the music of Abbey Lincoln, Joni Mitchell, and Nina Simone, which was released on the Resilience Music Alliance record label in January 2019. This album was selected by *JAZZIZ* magazine as one of "10 Jazz Albums to Listen To" in March 2019. It features vocalists René Marie, Alicia Olatuja, and Theo Bleckmann, guitarist David Rosenthal, pianist Allyn Johnson, and bassist Reuben Rogers in the band.

He is also excited to begin his journey as an author of books concerning music instruction, jazz drumming techniques, and entrepreneurship, the first of which is this book.

Ulysses remains consistently in demand for new projects as an artist, producer, and educator in addition to being one of the most sought-after drummers and thought leaders of his generation. Even though he has achieved measurable success, what consistently matters to him is giving back, continuing to be grateful, and seeking to make a difference in the lives of others.

Introduction

One of the joys of my childhood was when my father would reward me for good behavior like completing chores or doing great in school with a trip to the music store. Because my parents were on a fixed income, going to the music store was exactly one of those joys. It entailed me getting lost in the drum section and looking at accessories and drum kits for hours while my dad watched. The two stores I would visit in Jacksonville, Florida were Pro Music and American Music Store. I remember looking up at the counter near where they kept the drumsticks and seeing a pair of brushes, and I wondered: "What on earth could these be utilized for? How are these even used?" They always piqued my interest because they were, as I liked to call them, "non-sticks."

I first heard the brushes on a CD when I was around 12 or 13 years old, but I wasn't really aware of the sound and the technique until I started studying with one of the most influential drummers and instructors in my life, Ricky Kirkland.

Ricky Kirkland

Ricky was a great drum teacher for me because he respected the fact that I grew up playing mostly by ear in the Pentecostal church, which afforded me a certain level of technique in addition to a natural God-given ability. He didn't see that as problematic, and he would often tell me, "Ulysses, when you take a natural musician from the church and you educate them, then that is an unstoppable formula. And that's what we are going to do with you." He taught me how to read drumset charts in addition to the theory and history of the drumset.

My parents had already secured a classical percussion teacher from the Jacksonville Symphony along with drumset instructors and a classical piano instructor to build my fundamental understanding of music. Prior to working with Ricky, I had never encountered a jazz drumset teacher before. Through him, I also became informed about drum products and how they were made.

Ricky also taught me what true artistry and showmanship was like on the drumset. When you watch him play, it's like watching a movie. He loves every minute of being on the drums, so much that even if you aren't a drummer, you will fall in love with the craft by witnessing his love in action.

Ricky took me through various drumset and snare drum books when it came to technique and using the drumsticks, but I'll never forget that day when it was time to learn the brushes. I walked into his studio like normal, but instead of sitting in front of the drumset, Ricky sat me down and said, "I am going to teach you about the brushes." He showed me the kind of brushes he used at the time, and he wrote down the name of a pair that my parents needed to buy for me, telling me why I needed those specific kinds of brushes. He then sat me in front of a snare drum, showing me the technique and sound that I should strive for. That day began both a journey and love for the brushes that started from the time I was 14 years old, and the techniques Ricky showed me have remained with me throughout my entire career. Ricky showed me the method, and this allowed me to have a decent understanding about the sound of the brushes until my freshman year of college.

The next encounter with a brush master was when I studied with Lewis Nash. I moved to New York City to study with him at the Juilliard School as one of two drummers out of a hundred to be selected for the inaugural jazz studies program in August of 2001. Every time I would hear Lewis play the brushes live, on a record, or during the rare times he would invite me into the studio for a recording session, I would always be amazed by the distinctive sound and style that he possessed.

Lewis Nash

I was exposed to Lewis's sound partly because many jazz artists didn't travel to Jacksonville to perform. So the only way that I had an opportunity to know who was playing on a high level was by listening to records. I couldn't afford to buy a lot of records, so my friend told me about the public library in my neighborhood. I started going there to check out CDs and listen to them, and it was there I found a J.J. Johnson record called *Let's Hang Out* that featured both Victor Lewis and Lewis Nash. I remember hearing that sound of Lewis's drums, and I was instantly transfixed and addicted to the clarity and power of his performance.

Kenny Washington

Toward the end of my time in college, I studied with Kenny Washington, the so-called "Jazz Maniac" and foremost historical authority on bebop drum history. He began to show me brush techniques as Papa Jo Jones and Eddie Locke had shown him. He made a few adjustments to my approach, and it increased my overall sound on the brushes, allowing me to play with more confidence. Studying with Kenny was especially transformational because he was "old school" in his approach, and he didn't mince words. It was very much, "It's this way or the highway," not said arrogantly but more of, "If this is what you want to learn, then this is the jazz tradition, and here's how you learn it." I valued this approach greatly because it made everything more realistic for me. It was incredibly deep and meaningful for me to hear someone say, "Papa Jo showed me this, and now I am showing you." This proves that music is affective when passed down as an oral tradition from the master to the student.

As a performer in the last few years, I have been really fortunate to work with a lot of great artists, but one of the most highly regarded musical associations I have had was with the Christian McBride Trio featuring Christian McBride on bass and Christian Sands on piano. Throughout the touring and recording of this trio, it was our collective goal to create a sound that was steeped in the jazz tradition, yet had a forward and present approach that was relevant to current audiences.

McBride would come up with arrangements on the spot during sound-checks at gigs, and I remember at every concert, he always made a point to perform several songs where I would be featured on the brushes. I recall him saying to me one time, "Young cats don't really know how to play brushes anymore, but you do." So he started creating moments in the show to spotlight that part of my playing.

As YouTube videos and recordings would surface around the world from our shows, I started getting emails and requests via social media asking me about my approach to the brushes. This picked up especially once the famous "Cherokee" video was released online featuring Christian McBride, Peter Martin, and myself in Slovakia with me playing fast swing time. All of a sudden, I was regarded as a young "brush guru." You can find the video on YouTube through these general keywords: "Christian McBride Trio Cherokee."

I have had a chance at this point to travel the world and teach many students, and one of the greatest definitive aspects of jazz drumming to me is playing the brushes. In my opinion, jazz is the genre that owns the sound of the brushes and has created the need for them. However, there are several different approaches to playing them. With many accomplished and highly regarded drummers still playing today, I try to inform all of my students about the technical way in which these masters approach the brushes.

One of the focuses that I have seen in previous publications has been on the many ways you can play the brushes in multiple genres and styles. I would like to actually present the history and fundamental patterns of playing the brushes as it relates to only jazz music. My hope is to create a way for students to truly begin to master these patterns and play time effectively in various ensembles. You can learn multiple things, or you can focus on one thing and truly set yourself apart from the masses with the accumulation of mastery in that area of focus and study.

When drummers have contacted me and asked about my technique as though it's something that is magical, I just take them back to what Ricky, Lewis, and Kenny taught me: what the past masters showed them. I tell each student that they have to study and perfect the craft, not just attempt to play the craft.

I have always said for many years that I would never write a brush book. This is because I honestly felt that I learned so much of what I know about jazz drums the old school way, or "the oral tradition," via recordings and by merely watching the masters play. This is still the most effective way to study this tradition. However, during my travels, I realized that so many people around the world want to know how to correctly approach this art form with respect to the early jazz tradition. Also, from a current perspective and regarding this new generation of drummers, I felt there needed to be an updated resource solely about the brushes. This book is my attempt to create a viable tool for drummers around the world.

Social media is a really cool tool if it is handled in the right manner. Within the last year, I have posted a few videos of me playing basic jazz time with the brushes, and the responses have been incredibly overwhelming, not just from people being complimentary of my playing. It was also interesting to me how many people really wanted to see an up-close example of how to play the swing brush pattern. This made me realize that there needs to be some new examples out there that point drummers and enthusiasts to the history and application of this art form of brush playing.

Again, my desire in this book is to focus truly on playing the brushes in a jazz context by understanding the history, method, and application via analyzing the form and style of the masters.

Let's dig in and swing!

U

Information Concerning Audio, Video, and Additional Materials

This book has been designed to not only supply you with the information and tools necessary to develop your skills with jazz brush technique, but to give you additional instruction through recorded audio tracks and video clips featuring great arrangements tailor-made for this project.

The audio component of this book features an all-star group of New York-based jazz musicians playing with me on several tunes that cover a broad range of styles, tempos, and other elements. You can choose whether to play with my recorded parts on each track or to play with the rhythm section and vocalist without the recorded drums.

The video component features myself and a former student of mine, Aaron Jennings, working through some of the techniques and difficulties that drummers can encounter while learning the brushes. Part 5 of the book goes into greater detail concerning how to learn specific concepts relating to tempos, styles, time signatures, and rudiments in addition to trading phrases and a bonus interview with Aaron.

Most of the tracks and clips have accompanying notation examples that provide you with a written representation of the concepts and techniques discussed throughout the book.

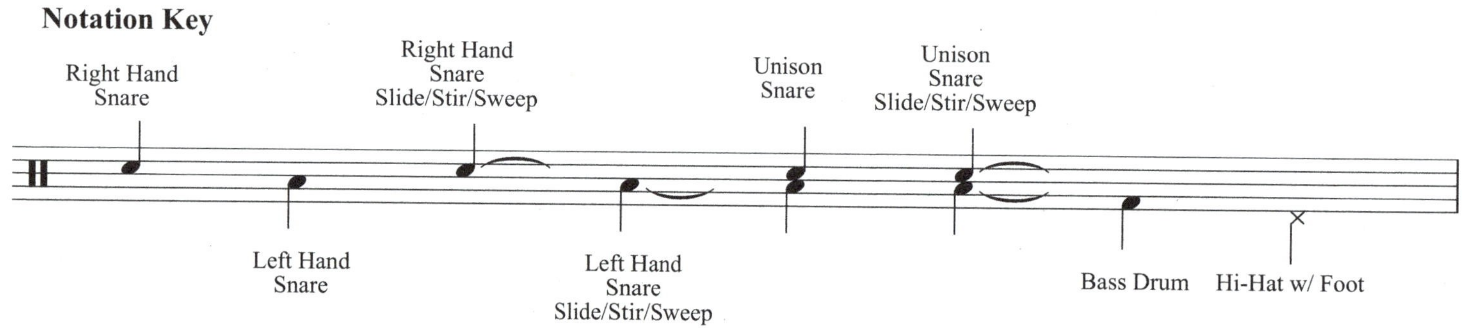

An additional feature that is included in this book is a collection of transcriptions of my most popular brush solos. These transcriptions have their own notation legend at the top of the first page, using the same symbols that appear throughout the book but accommodates for the rest of the kit.

All supplementary materials can be found on *halleonard.com/mylibrary/*, where you can input the code printed on the first page of this book to gain full access to audio, video, and written music to aid you in your journey playing jazz brushes!

PART 1: The History

CHAPTER 1: What Are the Brushes and Why Do We Need Them?

The brushes are a pair of drum accessories that can be used to strike/play a drum, and they are typically constructed with an internal metal rod, gum rubber grip, and retractable wire bristles. Ed Thigpen excellently describes them in his article "The Beauty of Brushes":

> "Most brushes are made with thin- to medium-gauge wires attached to a light metal rod encased in a handle, also made of metal, covered with rubber or plastic. This type of brush is usually retractable. Some brushes are non-retractable, being attached to a wooden handle for the purpose of having a sort of brush and stick combined. There are also brushes made out of plastic. Each type has certain advantages in different musical situations. I have found brushes made with thin-gauge wire offer the broadest range of possible sounds. This is due mainly to the flexibility of the wires."[1]

How Are the Brushes Used?

Historically, the brushes originated within the jazz genre of music, and they have been used to play on song forms such as ballads with small jazz groups, piano trios, and jazz vocalists. They have also been instrumental in musical scenarios where the volume was a concern, such as in silent films and vintage radio broadcasts. They have typically been played on the snare drum or hi-hat by various drummers. Today, they are used in multiple contexts by modern jazz drummers and drummers playing varying musical genres.

Who Makes Them?

There have been over a dozen companies to date that have made their version of the jazz brushes, and some of those companies are: Regal Tip, Brushworks, Slingerland, Vic Firth, Vater, Ludwig, Innovative Percussion, and Pro-Mark, to name a few.

It's important to know that much of the early jazz music before the 1950s has multiple sources and accounts of what happened, where, and when. However, when referencing the 1920s–1940s, it's important to know that, despite the recordings that exist, there are still many great musicians who may have never even been recorded, yet still made a significant contribution to the music and the art form of the brushes.

Particularly in the early days of jazz before recording technology had an opportunity to catch up, there were many musicians that were masters of this art form of brushes, and they played with multiple artists, some for a living. Due to the lack of exposure of their talent, some people got the credit and others did not. It is my desire to not only represent those that are famously known as great brush players but also those who are under-represented in the art form.

1 Ed Thigpen, "Jazz Drummer's Workshop—The Beauty of Brushes," Modern Drummer, October 1982.

Why Do the Brushes Need to Exist in Music?

The first iteration of the brushes was actually in the early 1900s using fly swatters on the snare drum. In the early days of recorded music, the microphones could not handle the sound of the drums hit with sticks. Early musicians are mentioned using the fly swatters (which were much smaller then compared to now) to play the early swing pattern on the snare drum. This allowed proper time-keeping support at a low volume.

New Orleans, Louisiana is noted as the birthplace of jazz music, and this music derives directly from the descendants of African slaves. This music also comes from the struggle that created the true creative spirit of people of African descent. Many New Orleans drummers were incredibly instrumental in the evolution of jazz music and the art form of the brushes because the music was created there. Moving from New Orleans to Chicago, New York, Philadelphia, and many other cities around the United States and the world, this music grew and is still maintaining its impact and presence over 100 years after its inception.

It's important to know that you can't speak about the brushes and the necessity for their existence without speaking about the reality of the recording industry and technology at the time.

There were two different types of recording technology present in the early days of jazz: acoustic and electric recording. Acoustic recording involved capturing the sound of live bands into a conical horn. All of these recordings did not have drums because the horn could not handle the vibration and sound of the drums. In 1926, electric recording became possible using a microphone that could actually pick up quieter sounds along with an early version of a mixing console. The electric recording process could capture quieter sounds such as a fly swatter, but it still had trouble with vibrations just like the acoustic recording horn. Therefore, the whole kit could not be recorded until later. The whole drumset itself was not able to be recorded successfully until the late 1920s. Before that, the recording configuration typically involved a banjo, horn, tuba, and drummer playing a woodblock or another piece of percussion. This was the extent of what the recording technology could handle.

What's for Dinner?

With this information above, the need for the brushes in early sound recordings and film was beyond necessary. Also, it's important to know that in addition to the recording technology limitations, there were also issues around the audience development at that time. This is a fancy way of stating that most people just saw the music as an accompaniment to a nice dinner or party. Drummer Joe Calato put it this way: "You pick up a pair of sticks, and you would get fired. This was the era when people came to dinner, and they wanted to talk."

CHAPTER 2: The Brushes and Jazz Music

Saxophonist Steve Wilson once said to me that legendary jazz saxophonist Jackie McLean told him, "All new music is behind us." What I take from his words is that everything we will have in the future can be most truly understood by the proper study and deconstruction of the past. Jazz music has many eras, but the two that I want to focus on revolve around the early jazz period and the swing jazz era.

Rhythmic Patterns of Early Brush Players

It's important to know that as the patterns of brush playing started to evolve throughout the pre-1940s, many of the drummers used simplified rhythmic patterns in the music before the well-known "spang-a-lang" pattern was widely and unanimously utilized.

Many of the early brush players literally played simple time with variations of the quarter note and, in many ways, modeled the rhythms coming from the banjo. You will also notice in many early jazz recordings that it's difficult to even hear the sound of the brushes over the banjo, because at the time, it was the primary source of keeping time within the ensemble.

Drummers played with rhythmic variations that included either a variation of quarter-note back-beat time with the emphasis on beats 2 and 4, or on all four beats.

Gerry Paton wrote a great piece for BrushBeat.org called "Early Jazz: Styles for Brushes," explaining the evolution and creation of the brushes in jazz music, which I highly recommend to anybody to read.

Here are some illustrations and notated examples of the basic mechanics of using the brushes along with the bass drum and hi-hat.

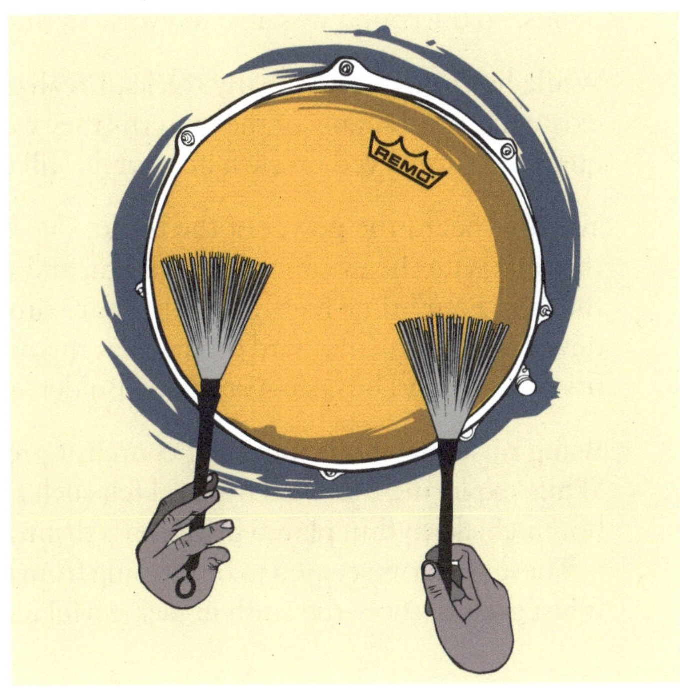

Bass Drum on 1 & 3

*Please use both brushes for exercise above.

Bass Drum on 1 & 3

*Please keep the slide patterns in time.

Bass Drum on 1 & 3

*Accent left and right hands on beats 2 and 4.

I have divided recordings from the early brush players and the evolution of the sound of brushes into three periods: the 1920s, 1930s, and 1940s. Each decade allowed for a different approach to the brushes while also introducing new possibilities with the evolution of recording technology and music stylings, as mentioned earlier.

The Evolution of the Brushes in the 1920s

In the 1920s era of jazz, the brushes showed up on the scene and were primarily used as a tool to keep time in a simple fashion, mostly revolving around a lot of quarter-note legato phrases. Many of the best drummers of the time from New Orleans and Chicago were playing brushes in multiple bands, so the sound was able to evolve in the hands of the best.

While listening to these early tracks, I realized that the spang-a-lang pattern wasn't technically in existence, yet so many of the patterns they were playing were similar to either a backbeat feel or to quarter notes played on each beat while still emphasizing beats 2 and 4 with accents.

You also heard the power of the banjo, slap bass, and tuba sharing the pulse and commitment to the time with the drummers of this era, and you can definitely hear the New Orleans emphasis on the "Big Four" time-feel. The "Big Four" time-feel refers to a syncopated bass drum rhythm that deviates from the standard on-the-beat rhythm played in marching bands around the time that jazz first emerged. (The cornetist Buddy Bolden is credited with inventing this.)

Being raised in the Pentecostal church, I grew up with a style of song we call "shouting music." While exploring these old tracks, I felt such a clear connection between shouting music and a fast, boom-chick rhythm played by the bass drum on beats 1 and 3, with the snare drum on beats 2 and 4. These patterns seemed to be echoing from the early jazz age, vibrating right into the 21st century. It just goes to show the truth in Jackie McLean's words, "All new music is behind us."

Select Recordings from the 1920s

Andrew Hilaire with Jelly Roll Morton, "Grandpa's Spells," 1926.

One of the first sound recordings of the brushes featured the dynamic New Orleans-born drummer Andrew Hilaire. On this recording, I was quite puzzled because I was convinced Hilaire was using sticks until I really focused and listened to the rhythm coming from the slap bass and banjo. It wasn't until the brush fill at 1:30 that I was convinced he was playing brushes, and he sounded so good. This track reinforces the notion that during this period, drummers, especially those with brushes, just kept time. Check out that great bass drum feel he has going on as well.

Andrew Hilaire

Warren "Baby" Dodds with the Jelly Roll Morton Trio, "Wolverine Blues," 1927.

Baby Dodds was from Chicago, which is where this next song was recorded with the Jelly Roll Morton Trio. On this recording, the brushes come in around 1:35, and Dodds focuses mainly on playing the bass drum and then playing on the hi-hat in the first chorus. On the second chorus, he opens up and plays more of a backbeat feel. Just listen to the way he orchestrates around the drumset so effectively, not just playing time on the snare drum but really creating an arrangement.

Warren "Baby" Dodds with Jelly Roll Morton's Red Hot Peppers, "Beale Street Blues," 1927.

On this track, Dodds really drives home the backbeat feel with brushes. He amazes me with the level of groove and commitment to the time-feel, almost like a predecessor to the funk drummers. He is keeping seriously focused time!

Johnny Wells with Jimmie Noone, "Monday Date," 1928.

Johnny Wells was on the list of drummers whom I had not encountered before writing this book. I discovered he was a fixture on the Chicago jazz scene in the '20s and '30s and very influential to some great drummers who received more credit for their playing than he was ever fortunate enough to receive in his lifetime, which would include Gene Krupa and other notables of the era. In his terrific autobiography *Really the Blues*, Mezz Mezzrow writes that he and Gene Krupa would sit for hours beating out the rhythms of Zutty Singleton and Johnny Wells "...until [his] hands swole double."[1] On top of his drumming, Wells was also known at the time as a singer, dancer, and comedian.

On this particular recording, Wells and Noone are playing at a brisk tempo, and you can't quite find the brushes until around 1:00. You can hear the brushes peeking through sonically, and Johnny Wells is playing a steady quarter-note pattern around a backbeat feel. Notice how his time-feel shifts when the tuba becomes more of the driving force in the track, which is where he starts to let the banjo take more control. Also, note how Wells switches to sticks toward the end of the track as the volume of the ensemble increases and more is needed from him dynamically.

1 Mezz Mezzrow et. al. Really the Blues (New York: New York Review Books, 2016), 157.

Select Recordings from the 1920s

Tommy Benford with Jelly Roll Morton's Red Hot Peppers, "Shreveport Stomp," 1928.

Tommy Benford is another talented drummer who I became aware of only through writing this book. Tommy was born in Charleston, West Virginia, and he began working with the great Jelly Roll Morton on the Green River Minstrel Show. On the recording that I chose for this section, you can really hear the influence of groove playing in his approach to the brushes.

The recording quality is much better than the earlier recordings of this track, and Tommy plays a heavier backbeat. He is also using more drum fills than his predecessors, keeping strong time on all quarter notes with very little deviation. He then switches to the top cymbal during the clarinet solo to add a different color.

This track is a significant foreshadowing of brush playing to come in terms of orchestrating the brushes around the kit during solos.

As fate would have it, during my research I realized that the grandson of Tommy Benford, the young and talented drummer Kyle Benford, was one of my students at the Juilliard School. Again, we see that when we look to the future, we can find the past.

Kaiser Marshall with McKinney's Cotton Pickers, "Miss Hannah," 1929.

Kaiser Marshall is another early drummer who deserves more of a legacy than he's been given. Marshall hails from Savannah, Georgia. He had enough chops to study with George L. Stone and to work with Fletcher Henderson, Sidney Bechet, and Bunk Johnson, among others. On this recording, Marshall is playing in the Cotton Pickers band alongside Coleman Hawkins, Benny Carter, and Fats Waller. He uses the brushes with a vocalist and heavily emphasizes the use of his brush handle on the hi-hat. In this example, his playing doesn't really expand beyond this, and the brushes remain committed to keeping solid time for the band.

Buddy Gilmore

There are other great drummers worth mentioning from the 1920s who are rarely spoken about today, and though my focus is on brush players, Buddy Gilmore was a huge influence on all of these other talented drummers we've been discussing. Buddy Gilmore was a player from Raleigh, North Carolina, who apparently influenced a young four-year-old drumming sensation called "Traps the Young Drum Wonder," whose true name was Bernard Rich. It is rumored that Gilmore made such an impact on the boy that the young "Traps" changed his name. I am referring to, of course, the great Buddy Rich.

Buddy Gilmore was the first truly famous African American drummer of the 1920s. He toured with James Reese Europe throughout Europe, and he spent much of his life living there. He was what we would call today the first "superstar" on the drums and was featured in many early African American newspapers. His power on the drumset was admired by the masses, and he was revered by many musicians way before all of the other great drummer bandleaders would emerge.

Buddy Gilmore

The Evolution of the Brushes in the 1930s

This era saw the emergence of really wonderful brush players hitting the scene. Although they continued with the standard of keeping time, they were subtly but surely expanding their technique to make more musical and orchestrated choices with the brushes.

Select Recordings from the 1930s

"In the '30s when I would play, they didn't want to hear you, they wanted to feel you. My first brush teacher told me, 'You better have a good feel, or don't pick them up.'"—Joe Calato

Stan King with the Dorsey Brothers, "Breakaway," 1930.

You'll hear Stan King playing brushes during the piano solo on the last chorus. In his day, King was known as the "Busiest Session Drummer," playing with all the greats of the time.

When I listen to this track and others of the same time, I notice something fascinating: the drummers of the late 1920s and early 1930s were establishing what would become an "unwritten rule" to make sure brushes were always played under the piano solo. You can hear the continuation of that unwritten rule in the drummers of the 1950s, who would use a cymbal with rivets or a lighter cymbal, or even just change the timbre of their time-keeping specifically during the piano solo.

Harry Dial with the Alex Hill Orchestra, "Dyin' with the Blues," 1930.

On this recording, Harry Dial continues a traditional pattern similar to most of the drummers we've discussed of this era. You'll notice he's playing a lot of time with the top cymbal of the hi-hat for most of the song. Then during the piano solo, he brings out the brushes with the heavy quarter-note pattern emphasizing beats 2 and 4.

This is a stark difference from the drummers in the early 1920s who were merely playing quarter-note patterns. We can clearly hear the brush evolution in action on this recording moving from simple time-keeping to something more complex, perhaps even melodic.

Walter Bishop with the Dixie Rhythm Kings, "Story Book Ball," 1930.

Walter Bishop was yet another drummer from the Chicago jazz scene whom I had never had the privilege to hear until recently. But when I did, I recognized his deep connection to Jelly Roll Morton, Earl Hines, Sy Oliver, John Kirby, and many other great bandleaders and musicians.

On this particular recording, I started to see the consistency in this era with a few things musically. Walter is keeping great time, again with the quarter-note pattern on the snare drum with the brushes. It's interesting when the tuba is playing; he mostly plays on the hi-hat, which really speaks again to orchestration, even in this era. It seems to be common that when the tuba drops out, the drummer immediately picks up the brushes and plays softer to balance the sound.

Time-Keeping Options in Early Jazz

In the early days of jazz, drummers had a few different options of time-keeping with the brushes. It's interesting to hear how committed every drummer was to the orchestration during solos, making very similar choices on how they supported an ensemble:

1. With very little nuances beyond time-keeping, the brushes are played subtly during the piano solo, creating a solid pulse.

2. The ends of the brushes are played sometimes on the hi-hat during other solos, and the drums are consistently never loud on the recordings because of the technology.

3. When the drummer has an option to play the brushes, they are either playing the back-beat on beats 2 and 4 or playing quarter notes every beat with accents on beats 2 and 4.

4. Choking the top cymbal on beat 4 with the brush handle is used often at the end of a song.

The Evolution of the Brushes in the Late 1930s—Early 1940s

As the decades progressed, so did the style of the brushes, and it would eventually evolve into what is now considered artful brush playing. In the late 1930s, drummers who would one day be known as great bandleaders and innovators, like Papa Jo Jones and Gene Krupa, weren't merely keeping time anymore; they were starting to lightly embellish the time. What makes this brief period of time in jazz so cherished to drummers is the birth of the drum solo played with brushes. All of a sudden, you had drummers beginning the tune with a drum fill in addition to soloing after the other instrumental solos were complete, then heading back to the top of the tune. In my opinion, this is the era when drummers started to play more like they were being heard instead of just being in the background. This would be a foreshadowing of the great bebop drummers to come a decade later.

Select Recordings from the Late 1930s–Early 1940s

Jo Jones with the Kansas City Five, "I Know That You Know," 1938.

Within the first bar of the tune, you can hear a stark difference from the earlier recordings. First, Jo Jones starts the track with a drum fill played with the brushes, which can be heard clearly. It's the first time you hear a brush solo, and it's two choruses, which is unique and had never been heard in the 1920s, or even the early 1930s. Another novelty is Jo Jones playing the spang-a-lang pattern in the right hand, adding quite a few embellishments.

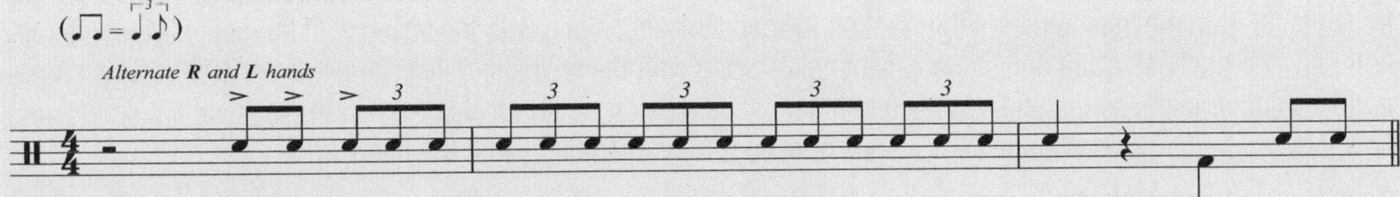

Gene Krupa, "Wire Brush Stomp," 1938.

Gene Krupa is dealin' on this track, and like "I Know That You Know," what amazes me so much is how the drums are now properly featured. You are no longer struggling to hear the brushes, and they are starting the track on the hi-hat. But here, Krupa is also referencing the style of the early drummers, like Zutty Singleton, Baby Dodds, and Tommy Benford, by playing strong quarter notes.

When the drum solo happens, you start to hear this beautiful addition of rudimental influences, a part of Krupa's signature style of playing. Clearly, a new day has dawned for the brushes on these two hot tracks. Krupa takes his solo, incorporating the floor tom, snare drum, and top cymbals, effectively flipping the entire approach from just one drum to using a whole set during the solo.

O'Neil Spencer with John Kirby, "Front and Center," 1940.

O'Neil Spencer is a really special drummer whose career was cut too short after contracting tuberculosis. In his brief life, Spencer influenced many drummers who went on to become famous after his death, and we'll give him his due here. It is said that Buddy Rich was a huge fan of O'Neil Spencer and I can understand why; it's because he plays some really beautiful rhythms on the snare drum. When you listen to Buddy on those *Ella and Louis* records, you can hear a true thread of where a lot of his brush vocabulary derives from.

> *"I learned about playing brushes from [O'Neil Spencer]. With those brushes, he caught the feeling and pulse of a hip tap dancer; his sound was clean and perfect."*—Buddy Rich.[1]

To me, Spencer is incredibly tasty and keeps the time steady, but adds some of these cool, quick triplet "ruff"-sounding fills that just makes the music feel exciting. But touching back to the past, he plays the brushes on the hi-hat to sharp effect while also playing on the snare drum and using variations on the backbeat. The history of brushes is especially heard in his sound through the timeless, subtle elegance of his playing.

He also begins to play a kind of shuffle fill with the brushes, which was a definite departure from the other drummers of this era, demonstrating his own signature style and language with the brushes. Check out the transcription of a few bars of his time-keeping below:

1 Burt Korall, Drummin' Men: The Heartbeat of Jazz, The Swing Years (New York: Oxford University Press, 2002), 323.

Select Recordings from the Late 1930s–Early 1940s

Big Sid Catlett with Ben Webster, "Just a Riff," 1944.

Sid Catlett's brush sound is so full and big on this recording, and it's just beautiful to listen to his approach. On this track with Ben Webster, Sid is laying down some nice medium time, and his articulation is so clear. He is playing the spang-a-lang pattern in the right hand. He also has cool brush fills on and off beat 4.

You can hear him playing the hi-hat on the upright bass solo, which coincides with the fact that jazz music has now transitioned from the tuba in the rhythm section to acoustic bass, along with the absence of the banjo. More interaction between the bass drum and snare is happening along with the soloists, unlike earlier in the 1930s. This shows a true evolution in the sound and approach to the brushes. The drummers have taken off the musical handcuffs, and now they are getting closer to the early stages of bebop, truly interacting with the band.

Catlett was a true talent who is recognized widely for his ability. In *Drummin' Men: The Heartbeat of Jazz: The Swing Years* by Burt Korall, Dr. Billy Taylor is quoted as saying, "It was impossible to play with [Catlett] and not feel the essence of jazz."[1] In that same book, Korall quotes Don DeMicheal as stating, "Catlett brought a more melodic concept to jazz drumming."[2]

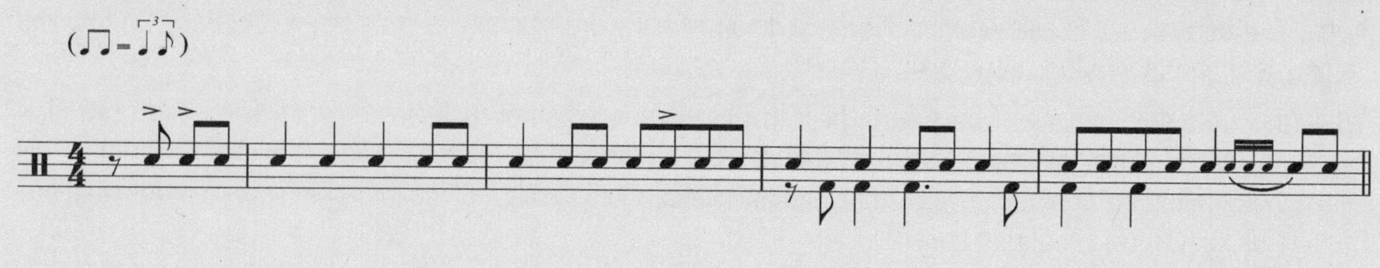

1 Burt Korrall, Drummin' Men: The Heartbeat of Jazz, the Swing Years (New York: Oxford University Press, 2002), 165.
2 Don DeMichael, "Evolution of the Jazz Solo," Down Beat (1961): 24–25, quoted in Drummin' Men: The Heartbeat of Jazz, the Swing Years by Burt Korrall (New York: Oxford University Press, 2002), 165.

All Drummers Keep Time

In my interview with Loren Schoenberg, jazz historian and Artistic Director of the National Jazz Museum in Harlem, I said to him, "What's fascinating to me, Loren, is that much of what I wanted to chronicle in this book is that some drummers started with just playing time, before they began to expand into more of an artful approach to brush playing." He corrected me and said, "Ulysses, *all* drummers started this way. There was no other approach or choice; everyone focused on keeping time because that was all there was for them to focus on."

My challenge to all of you is to venture back to the basics of keeping time and see if you can establish a few different ways of playing like the early drummers.

Exercise

Play time with the brushes using just quarter notes while also playing the bass drum.

Play time on the snare drum using only quarter notes while accenting beats 2 and 4.

CHAPTER 3: The Retractable Wire Brush

What Was the First Kind of Brush?

Much of what I learned about the evolution of the retractable brush came from an extensive interview for this book with Joe Calato, the founder of Regal Tip Drumsticks, Brushes, and Mallets. Calato secured the first patent for the retractable brush in 1960. From that day forward, he has been credited with making the first quality retractable wire brush with a black telescopic handle and metal wire bristles, and drummers immediately started using them. The demand for a well-constructed brush sent the business skyrocketing, and Calato's brush business boomed.

There were other companies making brushes before Regal Tip, most notably Slingerland, who made the brushes used by Gene Krupa and Buddy Rich in their early careers. In my interview with him, Joe Calato told me, "Brushes weren't being sold many places, because no one had created a comprehensive and quality model. I wanted to first make a good brush and one that felt good."

How Regal Tip Changed the Quality of the Brush

Sea Bruno, which was a distribution company for drumsticks, made Calato an offer: He would use their brush manufacturing equipment, and they would sell his drumsticks.

The equipment was old, but Joe used it while developing more equipment and started making his version of the brushes. Eventually, his own machines would update the brush quality, even employing an assembly-line approach with a dedicated team deciding how many wires to add to each brush and how to cut them. I got to see Calato's brush manufacturing ingenuity with my own eyes at Regal Tip's facility near Niagara Falls, New York. Maintaining consistency and quality continues to be a huge focus for Joe, the Calato family, and the Regal Tip company.

There are a number of evolutions of the brush that Joe Calato can claim responsibility for, a few of which he did immediately when he started manufacturing them:

1. **The Wires:** Finally, drummers didn't have to worry about the wires sticking. He used an aluminum tube so that they didn't stick: a simple but masterful solution.

2. **Gum Rubber:** Calato devised the use of gum rubber. This innovation was key because now the brush wouldn't cut the rubber when playing rim shots.

3. **Metal Wire with Stopping Points:** The wire had notches on it so that you could explore different adjustment points.

4. **The Brush Interior:** He redesigned the brush with a simple yet effective modification so that metal wouldn't hit metal.

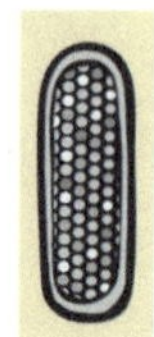

5. **The End of the Brush:** He tightened up the loop to prevent it from catching on players' sleeves.

Other Kinds of Brushes

Once Joe Calato created the Regal Tip 583 model in 1975, it quickly became the standard that many other companies referenced. Calato went on to create various other kinds of brush models, including special-order signature models for various players who had specific needs and requests.

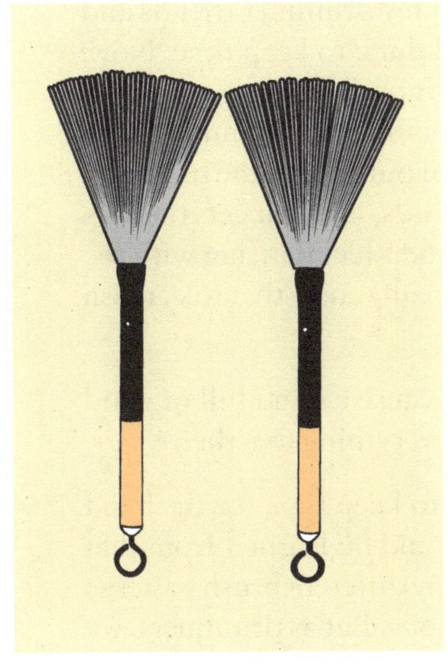

Regal Tip 584W

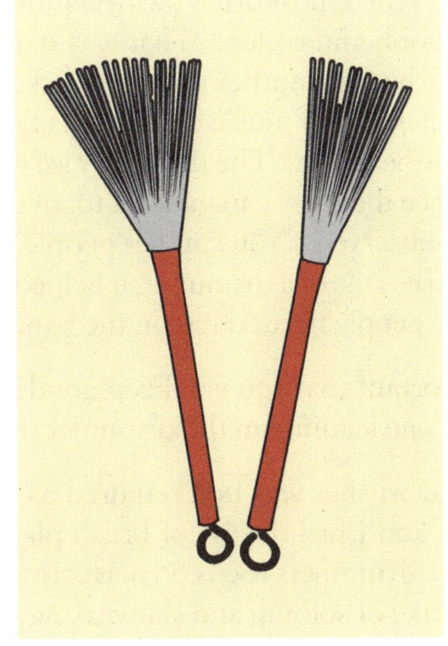

Regal Tip 583R

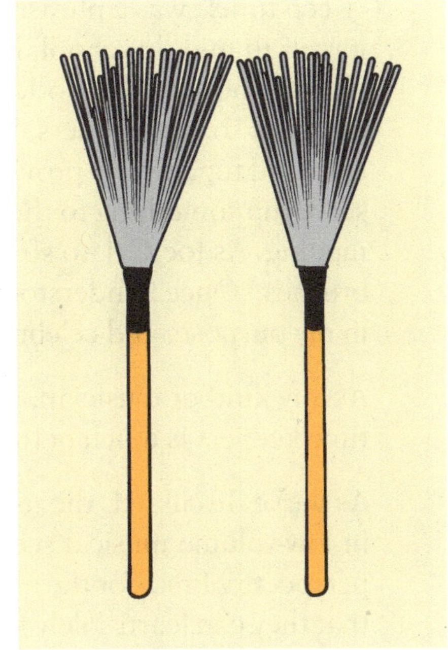

Regal Tip 550W

Do I Have to Use Only Brushes to Get the Right Sound?

At this point in the 21st century, a wide variety of drum accessories have been created to provide additional ways for musicians to get multiple sounds, textures, and timbres out of the drums. But the brushes are still a complete category by themselves with a long, rich history and a lineage of drummers who have created an entire vocabulary for the brushes in jazz music.

When I first was introduced to Hot Rods and wands, I could see they gave me the opportunity to create some interesting and different textures. However, brushes remain unique; there is a completely different approach to the snare drum and kit that is necessary to play them.

Ed Thigpen was one of the first jazz drummers to create a plastic Blastick, which he did with the help of Joe Calato. As the story goes, Thigpen provided the template and Calato had the prototype made in minutes. A Blastick features long, plastic bristles from either a wooden or synthetic handle that allow you play in a similar manner to a normal drumstick, but with a softer, yet still full sound. Much like the retractable wires on standard brushes, Blasticks feature movable rings on the bristles that allow you to adjust your sound to any given playing situation. This comes in handy when you want to play hard, but not overpower the band.

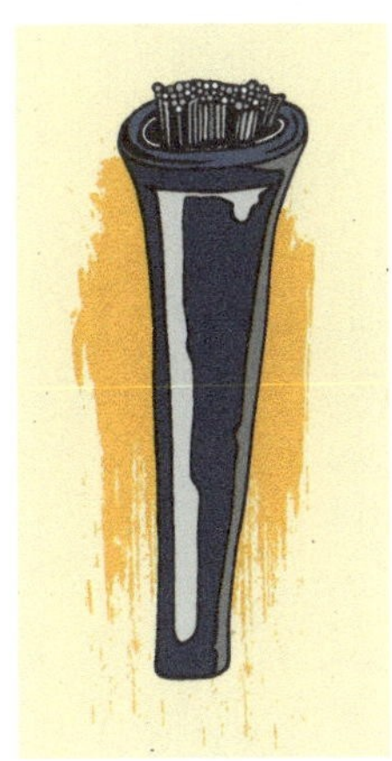

However, it's still worth saying: to achieve the proper sound of the brushes on the kit and snare drum, you need to use wire brushes, not alternative types of products. This is especially important when you are playing swing time in jazz as it will be difficult to accomplish that sound with anything but a real brush.

CHAPTER 4: The Necessity of Keeping Time

What Is Our Primary Role Within the Music?

Answer: *to keep time.*

"Keep time!" was a phrase I heard yelled most often by my bandleader at my drummer friends and myself in middle school, high school, and college. That was our sacred duty: to keep time. Now, this was not totally at odds with what my mother said my God-given gift of drumming was to be used for: to serve others. In the majority of music genres, it is fair to say that the drummer keeps the band together by providing the heartbeat. The drummer serves a vital purpose in the band and serves up something to the audience that they can grab on to. In other words, it's what gets the toes tapping. As Joe Calato so rightly observed, "You can get people up on their feet dancing with the brushes." Once I understood the true role of a drummer, it helped me to really enjoy that role, relish in my purpose, and celebrate why people needed me on the bandstand.

As any kind of musician, it's important that you can keep good time because a band full of good time-keepers is much better than one leaning on the drummer to keep everything together.

As we've discussed, the use of the brushes was first required as a need to keep time for the band in low-volume musical scenarios, and I feel the art of brush playing should be learned from that perspective first. For the most part, drummers focus on perfecting as many different brush patterns that they can learn solely for the sake of soloing and showcasing their chops. But as drummers, we must never forfeit our time-keeping responsibility. We must cherish it because it is at the heart of our purpose in the music.

There is one particular pattern that, if mastered, can become the rhythmic base of an ensemble and allow them to soar. As drummers, we must ensure our technique has the right focus to create what the ensemble needs. If the entire band is utilizing the right technique and musicality as their focus, then that is when the music is really going to be something special and pull an audience in closer to listen.

Please learn and practice the basic time pattern below:

* Play the spang-a-lang pattern with the right hand while sweeping in the left hand with no accents.

CHAPTER 5: Jazz Ensemble Configurations

Piano Trio

There are many different musical configurations within the jazz genre, but I will focus on just the fundamental ensemble groups, discussing their importance, how their music was created, and how it has been evolving since.

Even in some of the earliest jazz recordings I have on my 1920s playlist in Chapter 2, the configuration of piano trio can be heard. Some of my favorite piano trio records include superb brush playing. The few instruments of a trio meant the brushes had a chance to really shine, unless one of those three is a horn. When playing with a horn player, it can be challenging to hear the brushes (unless it's a ballad) because of the volume.

When playing within a piano trio myself, I typically have a goal to firstly, of course, "keep time!" Whether I am playing a jazz standard or an original tune, it is especially important to consider the type of music the ensemble is playing to help define the style in the song. Something else I love with a piano trio is that I can use space and play with silence as another instrument. Once your basics are tight, then you can truly have fun with your musical choices, which is something that never stops being a thrill.

When it comes to the brushes in a piano trio, I treat the roles of each hand just like I do while playing the drumset with sticks. My right hand is used as if I'm playing the ride cymbal, and my goal is to make that rhythm feel so good to the pianist that they feel supported, gliding along into each phrase beautifully. Also with the right-hand pattern, I want it to lock up with the acoustic bass player while they are walking bass lines. I treat my left hand just like the left hand of the snare, comping and locking in with the piano rhythms.

It is also important to have the freedom to be able to play consistent and driving time with the brushes solely, with or without the hi-hat—which would be played on beats 2 and 4.

The Vocalist

Early on in my jazz career, I realized that if I wanted to work often, then I would need to learn how to play with singers because they have more work than ensembles. I have learned a tremendous amount from working with vocalists, and much of my playing is heavily influenced by those experiences. Growing up in church, I already knew how to play and work with gospel singers, but the exuberance of playing gospel music did not require me to have a delicate touch. I was surprised when I started playing with jazz singers that they constantly told me I was playing too loud. Everything changed when I began to work with jazz singers, and I still attempt to bring that kind of quality and vocal articulation to my playing whether or not I am playing with a vocalist.

Many of my early gigs, from the age of 16 into my early thirties, were corporate parties and playing at restaurants in the back of the room while people were dining. Many times, I would show up to the gigs with just a snare drum and brushes and play time, which really helped my technique, but it also meant I had to keep my sound in a supporting role to the flow of the room. Similarly, singers wanted me to figure out how to work with them to add to their musical set but not take over with my volume. So like a drummer in the 1920s with his brushes whisking out a soft rhythm to accompany a cocktail party, here I was, almost a century later, following their lead. Whether working a room full of conversation or playing under one vocalist, using the brushes can be the easiest way to accompany a singer and rhythm section by adding nice time-keeping at a low volume.

After playing with brushes and learning how to alter my touch on the drum kit to play at a softer volume, my career really took off with many singers—not just locally, but nationally, and then internationally. This soft touch continues to allow me to create and collaborate with uniquely gifted vocalists, and I never stop absorbing what each of these experiences can teach me.

I offer this challenge to any drummer: try taking just a snare drum, snare stand, and a pair of brushes to a gig. Your technique will truly be tried and tested on multiple levels. When you are learning how to accompany an ensemble and solo, you can't get better practice in examining your technique.

The Great American Songbook

There is nothing like the Great American Songbook, the definitive collection of songs from the 1920s to the 1950s, where all the great composers like Richard Rodgers, Oscar Hammerstein II, Lorenz Hart, Duke Ellington, Billy Strayhorn, and many others are represented by their best works. As a drummer, if you are going to perform with singers and musicians in the jazz genre, then it is here that you will find most of the songs that you will need to learn, including the melody, harmonic form, and varying tempos at which each piece can be performed. There are several brush patterns that work wonderfully with these songs, no matter the musical configuration that you play them in. These patterns will always be a great compliment to these songs.

Below you will find a few standard patterns that will work well for songs from the Great American Songbook. Also, on the play-along portion of the book, you will find songs to practice that utilize harmonic movements from basic standard song forms, which are helpful to work on.

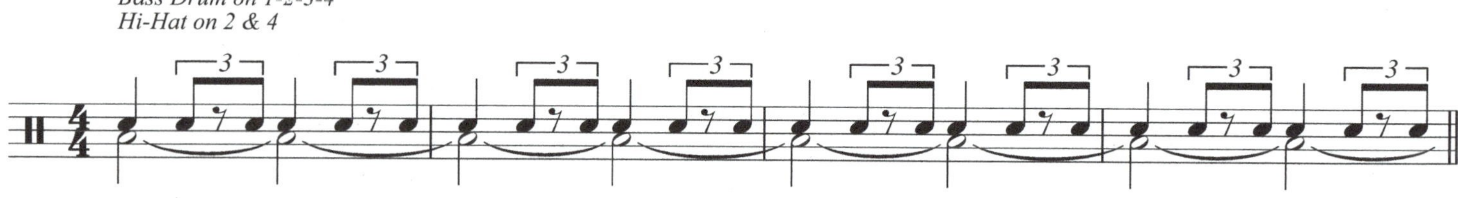

Play this example using the varying sweeping patterns below.

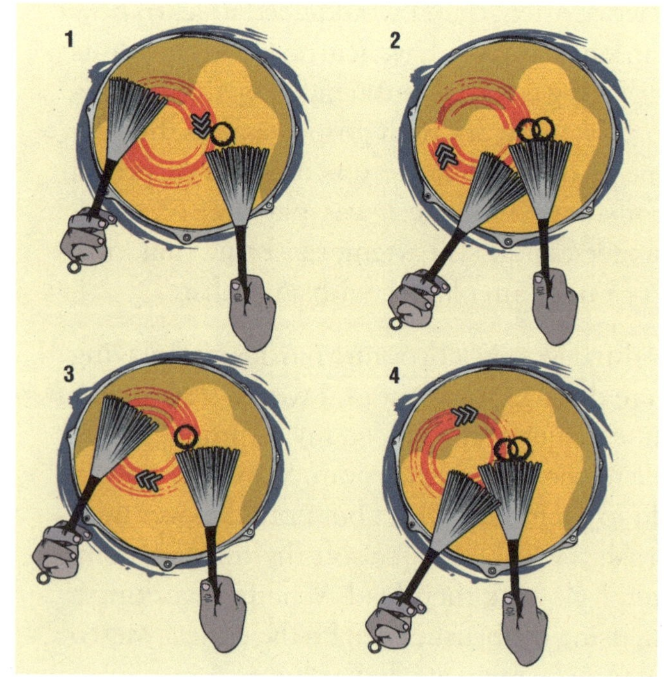

clockwise

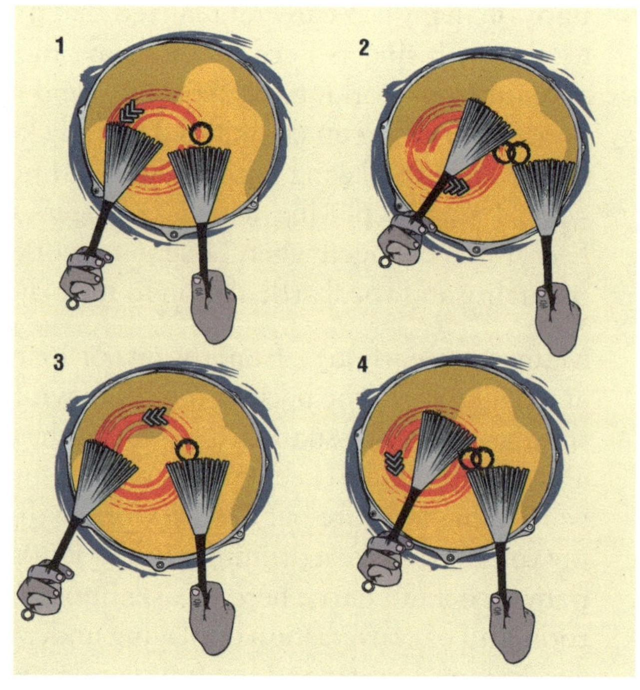

counterclockwise

Bass Drum on 1-2-3-4
Hi-Hat on 2 & 4

Play this example using the sweeping pattern below:

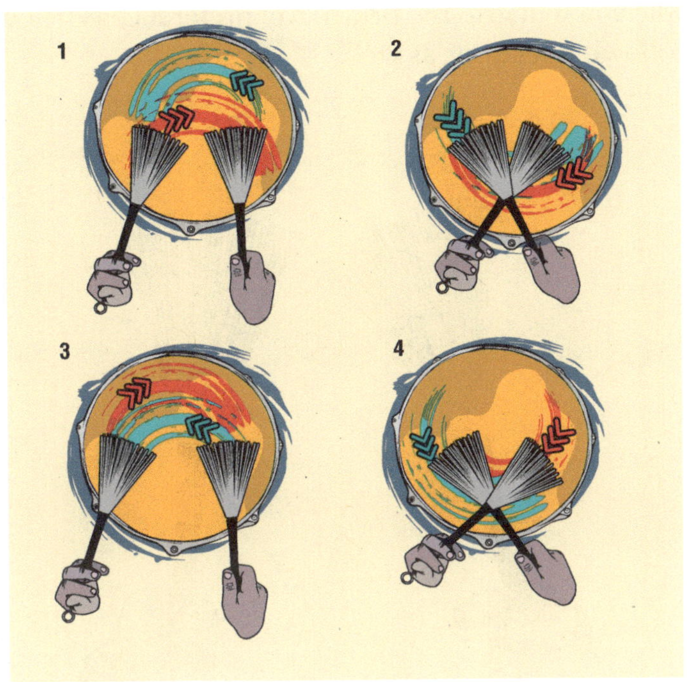

The Bass Solo

One of the questions I get from drummers constantly is simply, "What am I supposed to play during a bass solo?" I often tell them what the great bassist Ben Wolfe told me years ago.

I was accompanying him during a bass solo, and I was playing very bashful, trying to stay out of his way. He looked at me and said, "Man, give me what you give the horn players during their solo." I laughed and said, "But you play bass." He said, "I don't care, play for me so I have something to be inspired and solo over."

That's when I stopped playing in a timid manner and began to really use my brush technique to support bassists and give them a firm foundation.

During the bass solo, you can use the brushes on the snare drum and play the normal swing pattern softer, but be careful to not get in the way of the bassist and their ideas. My focus is to always make sure my volume during that time is under the bass, not overshadowing it.

You can also play the brushes on the ride cymbal or other parts of the kit to create a different timbre and quality for the bassist, but understand that during their solo it's about them, not you.

PART 2: The Method

CHAPTER 6: What the Hands Should Do

The Grip

One of the biggest mistakes I see a lot of young drummers and students make is based around wrong decisions with their hands, particularly how they choose to hold the brushes. In each hand, you must determine not only the type of grip, but also how loose or tight you will hold the brush, and how far up the handle you will grip the brush. My preference is below, and I have a few illustrated examples in the following sections as well:

Traditional vs. Matched

A point of contention, particularly amongst the new generation of drummers, is the matched grip versus traditional grip argument with brushes. Here is my truth and I am sticking to it: All of the masters of jazz played their brushes with a traditional grip. They used traditional grip because that was the original grip that most drummers used in the early jazz era. It's an interesting fact that many early jazz players learned drums from their drum and bugle corps days in military service, where they would have been taught to play with a traditional grip because of the nature of the types of drums used. Jim Payne discusses in *Modern Drummer* magazine that it was the military drummer's original purpose to lead soldiers forward in battle. The drummer would play while marching with a snare drum slung over one shoulder, which left the drum slanted in an awkward position to be hit with a matched grip, but an underhand grip worked. When drummers left the battlefield and were instead facing a drumset, they kept that same left-hand grip even though they didn't need to.[2]

2 Jim Payne, "MD Education Team Weighs in On: Traditional Grip," Modern Drummer, September 2009.

As interesting as that is, my thoughts are echoed best by jazz drummer legend George Marsh in this same article. When he's asked if drummers should play the traditional grip, his simple answer is, "...yes, if the student wants to play jazz." Marsh goes on to list the myriad of reasons jazz drummers should prefer the traditional grip, centering on the sound, the feel, and the attitude:

> *"Jazz is about feeling and attitude, and this difference in physical sensation [from the traditional grip] produces different music."*—George Marsh.[3]

In conclusion, as it relates to the brushes, if the ultimate goal of the jazz drummer is to echo all of the phenomenal cats before them and to honor and evolve the great jazz tradition, then we must use traditional grip. It's worth mentioning that it's very difficult to accomplish much of the left-hand technique without traditional grip. Having taught many students with both grips, I've observed that those using matched grip have to work really hard to get the left brush to articulate the correct movement. Of course, there are some exceptions to the rule, like the great Bill Stewart, who is an amazing jazz drummer and has such a dynamic sound using matched grip with the brushes.

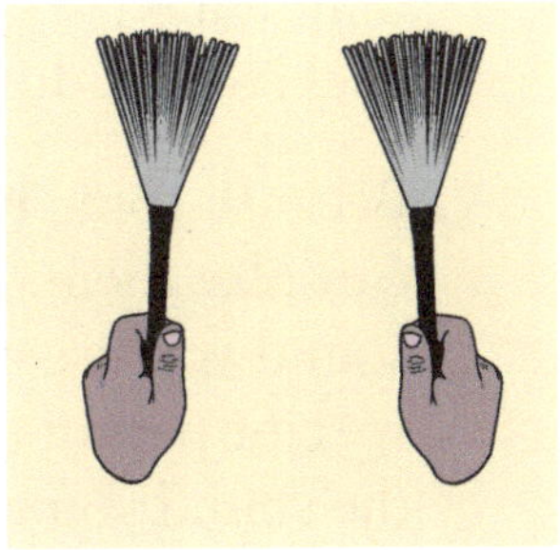

Right Hand

The spang-a-lang pattern comes from the triplet-based ride cymbal figure that was first used by bebop drummer Kenny Clarke.

Left Hand

3 George Marsh, "MD Education Team Weighs in On: Traditional Grip," Modern Drummer, September 2009.

CHAPTER 7: Height and Width of the Brushes

In my mind, Lewis Nash is the most innovative brush player alive; his ideas, velocity, and sheer virtuosity is second to none. He speaks with the brushes as clear as a beautiful sermon or eloquent poem. When I was first began to study with Nash, he took my brushes, held them in the air, wrapped his index and middle finger around the ends of the brushes and said, "This is the main part of the brushes you will always play." But, because brushes are not a standard height and width, that "main part" can create a variety of sound. A drummer's expertise will sharpen as they learn to wield all the differences.

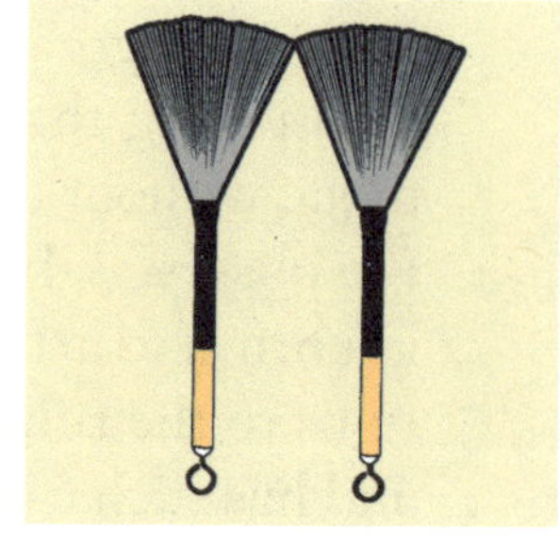

Because some brushes are retractable, there are multiple options of how you can play them. The height and width of the brushes determine much of the sound you are able to accomplish. Another variable is the positioning of the specific part of the brushes you utilize while playing time, which will also affect the sound you are able to achieve. If you're looking for the traditional sound, then play with the tips of the right brush and with the middle/meaty part of the left brush while playing the swing rhythm.

Height of the Brushes

Most of the drummers from the early jazz era only had a few choices in the height of the brush wires because manufacturing options were more limited than they are today. But now that we have so many options with our brushes, you should adjust the wires to a height at which you can control them and effortlessly play select brush patterns.

Width of the Brushes

When it comes to width, there is no set standard for greatness, and drummers have their own preferences. Some players, like the great Vernel Fournier of the Ahmad Jamal Trio, utilized a small amount of the brush bristles, yet got such a large sound. Louis Bellson used a wide fan on the drum and got a fantastic sound. Kenny Clarke, Papa Jo Jones, and many others played the drums with a medium fan, and you had better believe they got a great sound out of the drum!

Clayton Cameron, one of my favorite brush players, has been known to not only play effectively with a wide fan, but his signature brush doesn't have a retractable handle.

Retractable vs. Non-Retractable

There are many types of brushes on the market, but I personally feel that the best models are the retractable ones that reflect the vintage models that many of the jazz masters used. The retractable handle gives you an opportunity to control the height and width of your brush for various sounds and styles, which is a very helpful tool. In terms of durability and practicality, the retractable brushes won't get messed up as easily in the stick bag.

Height, width, retractable or not, there are so many options we are fortunate enough to have as drummers in the modern time. A good student will learn about them all—explore and feel what sits right with you, and make your own choices on how you will play the brushes.

CHAPTER 8: The Snare Drum and the Drumhead

When discussing the brushes, we must talk about the snare drum and the way in which you play it as a time-keeping element. Of course, the snare is not the only drum to play brushes on—you can apply brushes around the drum kit and get various sounds and timbres—but for time-keeping, it is superior.

I wrote earlier about the correlation between the banjo and the brushes in early jazz music. It is worth mentioning another major consideration for the brush pattern. When listening, you can hear a direct connection to the marching snare drum and the buzz roll patterns played in early New Orleans music that derived from the military rudiments. I truly think, because of the role the snare drum has always played in orchestras, marching percussion, and parade music, that the same focus remained when the brushes first emerged.

Snare Wires Off

Many of the jazz drum masters from the past actually turned the snares off while playing the brushes so they could gain a richer and fuller sound from the drumhead without leaning on the sound of the snare wires. It's vital to your sound that you practice the brush patterns with the snares off sometimes and with them engaged on others. It's even helpful to practice on other drums like the floor tom to really make sure that the technique is sound.

When I first learned the brushes from Ricky Kirkland, he instructed me to turn the wires off so I could really hear the sound of the brushes through the drumhead and the drum. It's the hard truth that when you have the snares turned on, it's easier to make the brushes sound good because of the vibration coming from the wires filling out the sound.

Snare Wires On

I occasionally like to play the brushes with the snare wires on, and it gives a nice clean, crisp timbre that can work well depending on the vibe of the music I am playing.

Types of Drumheads

For many years, I played with various types of drumheads on the snare drum because my focus was on using only the drumsticks. However, when you start to play the brushes more consistently, you will want to be cautious about the kind of drumhead you use.

Calfskin Drumheads

Drumheads have gone through various levels of evolution since the early 1900s, but it's impossible to talk about drumheads in jazz without mentioning the calfskin drumhead. The earliest drumheads were made from animal skin, particularly with the recordings from the early jazz era where the drummer played with brushes on calfskin. The sound of these drumheads was terrific, and honestly, I love the thickness and pure tone that comes from them.

However, these drumheads were incredibly temperamental. The tuning would change due to the weather because animal skin itself responds to the weather, expanding and contracting, particularly when the drum is being played in a warm climate. It became very difficult to have a consistent sound and tuning because of the nature of the calfskin drumhead.

As it pertains to playing brushes, the calfskin drumheads were ideal because the texture of the animal skin created such a great sound with the brushes.

Post-Calfskin Drumheads

In 1957 came the Mylar drumhead, first developed by Remo Belli and Sam Muchnik, which launched the Remo drumheads company. Remo offered a more consistent and less temperamental version of the calfskin drumhead called the *Fiberskyn* drumhead. The Fiberskyn is a great drumhead for brushes, and some of my favorite jazz drummers and brush players, like Lewis Nash and Jeff Hamilton, play this drumhead, and they get a great sound out of it. Personally, I am a big fan of the Remo drumheads. You can hold one up and just tap it with your finger and hear a beautiful sound.

When I would tour with Kurt Elling, we would run into a lot of the same bands on the road. Jeff Hamilton was someone I got to watch many times. But the first time I saw him play was at a *Modern Drummer* festival which was mostly full of rock, fusion, and funk drummers. On this rare occurrence, they included Jeff Hamilton playing with a trio. Boy, did he make so much music! But what stunned me the most were the Fiberskyn drumheads and such a small kit in comparison to all of these giant drum setups. Jeff sat down and played so much on the brushes that it erased everything else that I heard that night. Jeff Hamilton plays his brushes with class, precision, grace, and with a few tricks up his sleeve, making him a phenomenal player with jazz brushes. He has a high level of showmanship, and to put it simply: he can just play the drums. In my book, he is a must-see drummer should you ever get the chance.

I am a Remo artist, so I mainly use Remo Coated Ambassadors or the Remo Fiberskyn drumhead. The consistency of the craftsmanship is what has kept me coming back. I can always rely on the sound that my brushes will get with a Remo drumhead, and it's been this way for over two decades of my career.

No matter the brand of drumhead you choose to use, the most effective type for brushes will always be a coated drumhead to help generate a consistent sound. There are other great drumhead companies that make suitable drumheads for brush playing, so try a few out and see which one suits you best. Do not underestimate the importance of choosing the right drumhead, because without that detail, it will be next to impossible to have a great sound on the drum, no matter how great your brush technique.

Aquarian: Modern Vintage and American Vintage Drumheads. I used these drumheads years ago, and they are great for brushes.

Earthtone: Natural Skin Drumhead. This company offers a re-creation of the calfskin drumhead, and though I haven't tried it myself, I have heard great things about them.

Evans: Calftone Drumhead. I have played these, and they sound great for brushes.

Kentville Drums: Kangaroo Hide Drumheads. While writing this book, I became aware of a kangaroo hide drumhead made by the Kentville Drums Company in Australia. From the clips available, these drumheads seem to be great when played with brushes.

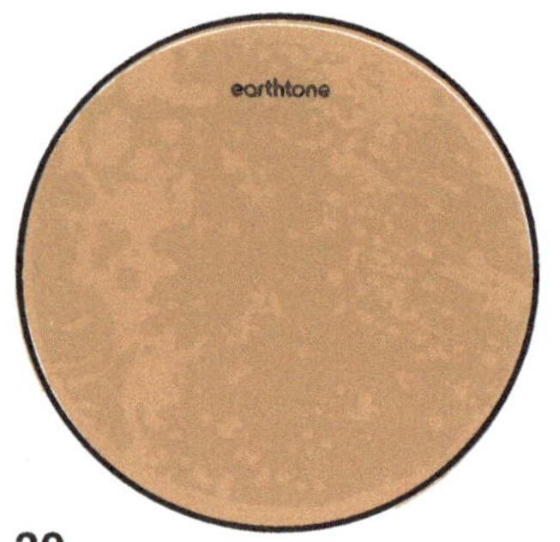

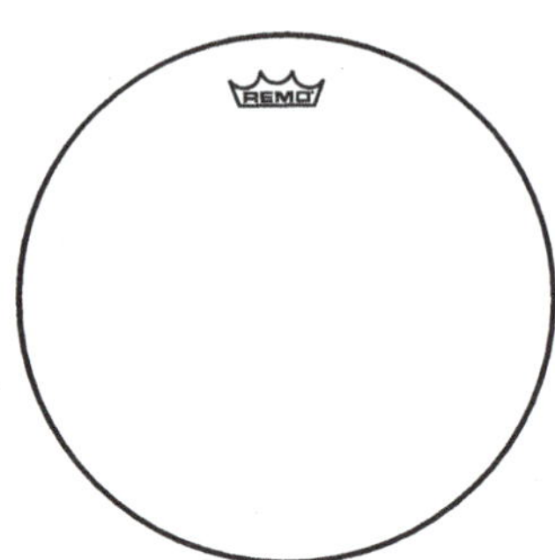

Breaking in the Drumhead

I have heard many methods on how to break in a drumhead effectively. Some use sandpaper to wear down the grating so that the brushes can have a smoother approach. I just use the brush to dig into the head with a few deep swipes to wear down the grating.

The Head Is Finished

Be careful that you monitor the shape of your drumhead, and make sure that you aren't seeing the mylar itself. If you see more mylar and clear coating and not enough white coating (or tan coating if it's a Fiberskyn), chances are you won't be able to generate a good brush sound.

CHAPTER 9: How to Play Good Time with the Brushes

The three major facets to music are melody, harmony, and rhythm. Most instrumentalists can properly cover two out of three of these qualities, but the rhythmic aspect of the music completely belongs to the drummer. In other words, it's our job to hold down the rhythm.

One of the major purposes of playing the brushes is keeping time for the rhythm section and vocalist. When Ricky Kirkland first sat in front of me with a pair of brushes, his goal wasn't to show me as many tricks as he could with them. Rather, he immediately started playing time with me, and I understood that should be my focus as well.

Often, when teaching a drum student, I ask them, "What is the role of the drummer in music?" They answer with many different things until I hold up my hand and say to them, as so many teachers have said to me, "Keep time!" Your priority and the heart of your mission as a drummer is to keep time, and with that, lay the foundation for everything else, which is no small responsibility. As a brush player, the goal is to get the time to feel so good that everyone can make better music because of you.

When I first started studying music, I understood that as drummers, our focus is mainly the rhythm, but not without understanding the other two elements of melody and harmony. As Lewis Nash always says: "Rhythm is our business." In fact, it was the title of his debut album! Every ensemble will always lean on the drummer to know where they need to be within the rhythmic aspect of every piece.

It is cool to truly understand what keeping time really is in jazz music. The primary rhythm in jazz is the swing rhythm, which is based around the triplet. The triplet rhythm is the foundation of the spang-a-lang ride cymbal pattern widely attributed to the playing of Kenny Clarke in the late 1940s bebop era. Typically in the swing pattern, the drummer will play it on the ride cymbal and the hi-hat on beats 2 and 4 while feathering the bass drum on all fours (quarter notes). However, when you keep time with brushes, you place both hands on the snare drum and isolate most of the time-keeping to the snare drum while still playing those patterns.

I remember when I first started playing brushes with various singers and musicians back in my hometown of Jacksonville, Florida. I was still in high school, and it was difficult for me to get my brushes to sound good. I know now that was largely due to my use of the wrong kind of brushes—an easy pitfall for any young player. But as they say, it's a poor workman who blames his tools. The other reason I was largely unsuccessful in creating the sound that I wanted was because I was focusing too much on the pattern and not the music. I wasn't tapping my foot and hearing the music in my head.

I have an experiment for you.

Sit in front of the snare drum and grab the brushes. Get a blues form in your head, pick a tempo, and start playing time. During the first set of 12 bars (first chorus), sing a melody while playing time. After that, during the second set of 12 bars (second chorus), sing the chordal movement. Finally, during the third set of 12 bars (third chorus), sing a walking bass line.

How did it go?

When you are able to play good time in sync with a metronome while simultaneously having the harmony and melody in your head, you are then truly ready to keep time and play with an ensemble. There is no greater achievement for a jazz drummer.

With the Hi-Hat

It's important to practice playing the brushes with a metronome with the hi-hat on beats 2 and 4 at varying volumes, and every player should learn both the heel-down and heel-up technique.

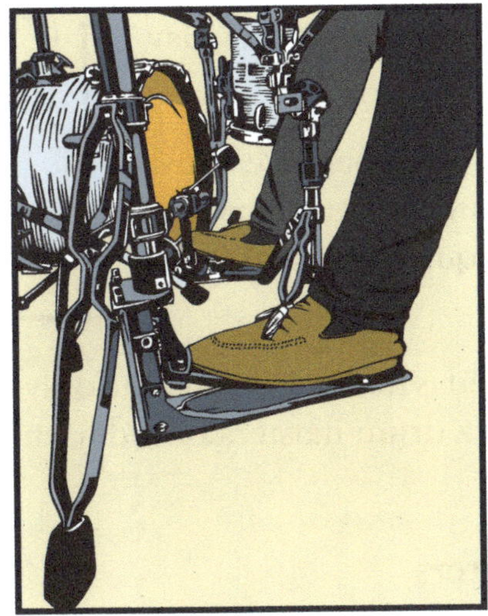

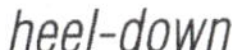

heel-down

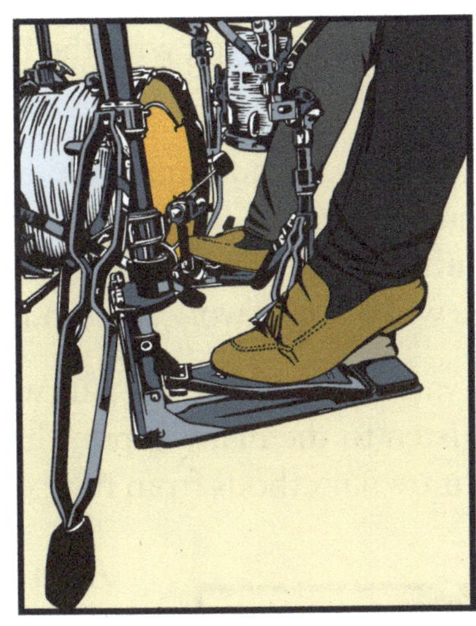

heel-up

Without the Hi-Hat

As we discussed with turning the snare on and off when you practice, it is imperative to also practice without the hi-hat on beats 2 and 4 in order to develop a solid and rich sound with the brushes. It allows you to hear how much time is really within your hands when the hi-hat isn't there to lean on for solid time-keeping.

The Center of the Drum: Why Does It Matter?

Many students get frustrated with me when I speak about specific places on the snare drum or kit and tell them to seek and consistently play those spots. This frustration leads them to wonder why there is a difference in their sound versus the sound of the jazz drum masters. Whether you are playing classical music or jazz, the sound you create on any instrument has everything to do with direction, proximity, and where you focus your energy and breathing.

Kenny Washington, the "Jazz Maniac," is one of the foremost authorities on bebop music and drum playing. Many of the masters directly passed on their knowledge to him, in addition to his own diligent study of their sound. The jazz masters anointed Washington in such a way that he has been able to teach the art form to many emerging drummers around the world. When I studied with him, the last thing that really elevated my brush playing was when I began to use the right hand to play the spang-a-lang pattern in the center of the drum. He also told me to reference the way I play that pattern on the ride cymbal, which is the part of the kit it was initially created for. Playing the right-hand swing pattern in the center of the drum really allowed my brush playing to have a more substantial and full sound.

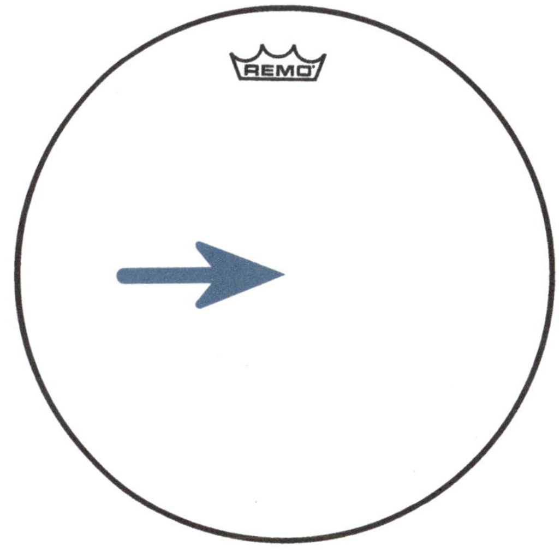

CHAPTER 10: Playing Ballads with Brushes

Move Your Arms Like a Ballet Dancer

Typically, playing ballads with the brushes is the only time most young drummers ever commit to playing with the brushes; otherwise, they normally play with sticks.

Being able to play ballads musically and successfully is rare because most drummers just resort to "floaty" and "busy" time. Learning how to move an audience with a beautiful ballad is a lost art, but if you acquire this skill, then many artists will want to work with you.

Developing variations of time-keeping while playing a ballad is important, and the only way to truly do so is to listen to the many approaches taken by the jazz drum masters of today and yesterday, forming your own methods from their examples.

Arm Movement Matters

The drums are some of the most physical instruments in the musical instrument family, and it's crucial to understand what your own body is doing when you play. Everything you do with your anatomy while you play will affect your posture and your breathing. This will ultimately affect how much you are able to accomplish on the drum kit, both stylistically and in terms of longevity.

After seeing the connection between how drummers and dancers use their limbs, lungs, and energy to create a graceful, fluid composition, I began a deep study of ballet. I could see the many ways ballet could inform the conscious use of my body as it pertains to playing the brushes with more ease, grace, and beauty. Some of my favorite drummers play the brushes with such elegance, and it is as much a pleasure to watch their movements at the kit as it is to listen to their sound. When studying the upper-body movement of ballet dancers—particularly when they were working at the bar and demonstrating first, second, and other fundamental positions—I noticed that their arms were in a circle extending beautifully in the same way that brush players move around the snare drum. I have found in my many years of teaching students that when I have them stand up to replicate ballet posture and positioning and then sit back down at the drum kit, they are able to achieve the right sound of the brushes immediately.

Sound Like the Ocean

When Lewis Nash began to teach me the brushes with a particular focus on playing ballads, he told me, "Sound like the ocean, Ulysses." The more that I forced myself to really sound like the calming seas, the more fluid my brush playing became. This technique involves each hand moving in position like a ballet dancer at a slow tempo to create that smooth, calming sound.

When playing a ballad, you should basically stir a pattern on each quarter note. The following music example shows you what to do:

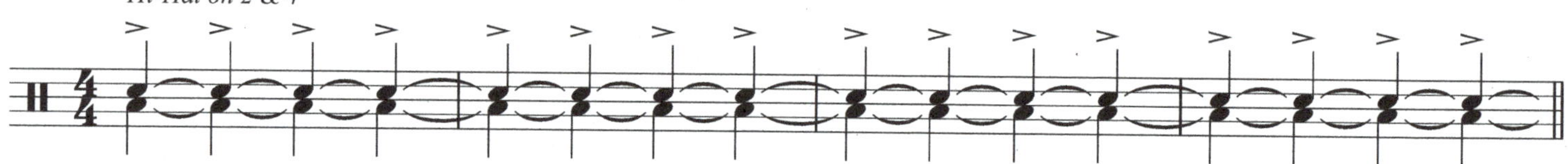

CHAPTER 11: Posture

The last two chapters focused on playing in the center of the drum, moving like a ballet dancer, and sounding like the ocean, all of which would be impossible without the necessary focus on posture. See the illustration below of what proper posture looks like:

Posture is one of the most important parts of playing any instrument more effectively, but many times, drummers make a lot of mistakes with this. As jazz drummers, it is all too easy to focus more on being stylistic in every facet of our playing while not necessarily understanding that great posture is at the very most fundamental basis of what keeps us going in a long career.

The reason dancers and athletes take such care to study anatomy, body movement, and kinetics is to keep their bodies as finely tuned machines that will sustain long careers of often grueling physical activity. This is equally true for many musicians. Good posture isn't just for athletes, dancers, or church; understanding and listening to our bodies can create a long-term career and enjoyment of the drums.

In middle school, I was very fortunate to begin learning classical percussion, and I played in orchestras and percussion ensembles until college. At that time, most of my understanding of posture had to do with studying techniques for classical snare drum, timpani, and mallet instruments, and this understanding has always stayed with me in my jazz playing. I would suggest that drummers work with a classical instructor, even if for a minimal amount of time, in order to understand proper posture and technique. No matter what instrument you play, studying some classical techniques can give more insight into your formal study and technique, creating a more natural flow with your use of the instrument.

During my first year at Juilliard, the administration created a schedule for all of the freshman students that exposed us to what is called Alexander Technique. The Alexander Technique was created by Frederick Matthias Alexander in the 1890s, and it has become a standard technique and philosophy studied by both actors and musicians to this day. To put it very simply, Alexander believed that the way we move in space and how conscientiously we conduct our physical bodies and breathing relates very directly to our happiness and success in our work as artists and even as human beings. Drummers should especially be aware of the Alexander Technique because—before even thinking about drums—our bodies are literally our instrument. Be sure to investigate this technique more in your own online research.

The Alexander Technique is not the only option for body mindfulness, but one way or the other, it is important to be incredibly tuned into your core, your breathing, your back, and the freedom of flow within and between your limbs. If there is restriction of breath or tension within the limbs when playing the drumset, then it will be difficult to get a good sound. This is especially true when playing the brushes.

The Power of Breathing

Any drummer that takes a private lesson with me sees first hand just how important proper breathing is to me as a teacher and player. It's always interesting to me when I meet a drummer who is maybe a little more uptight when playing than they realize—all of which is due to ragged breathing. Once I expose them to the power of proper breathing while they are playing, they laugh when they realize that their playing has so much tension because they just aren't breathing right—or sometimes aren't breathing at all. Make no mistake: when you don't breathe correctly, it affects your shoulders, then your arms, and then your wrists. I would argue that oftentimes, much of a drummer's difficulty on the kit comes from simply not breathing properly.

Here is an exercise I have all of my students try: I ask them to sit down and play in time while inhaling and exhaling. It's interesting to me that each player's sound always increases in volume on the exhale. That's an insight worth knowing, and you will discover more useful insights the more attention you pay to how breathing affects your patterns. I always use the drumstick to lightly touch the student's diaphragm to help emphasize the rise and fall of their chest with the rhythm of their breath. When a student is finally in-tune with the ebb and flow of breath entering and exiting their body, then their playing changes instantly for the better.

It sounds obvious, but sometimes the tricks to being the best player you can be are just simple personal choices like breathing while you play. I promise that it will help you. Tension comes from a lack of relaxation, but breathing gives relaxation to the body. This relaxation will add to your brush playing in multiple ways. Try it, and your playing will never be the same. It will always be better.

Seat Height

I often look back at old photos of my playing and marvel at all the many varying heights I've had on the drum kit until the last few years, during which I have been consistent with my seat height. Experiment with your seat/throne height because where you sit will affect how you hold the brushes and address the drums. Ultimately, the height of your throne helps dictate the sound you are able to accomplish.

When you are practicing the brushes, my suggestion is to isolate your drum throne and the snare drum/snare stand and practice with only that setup. If possible, I recommend getting a drum throne that has the spindle feature or hydraulics so that you can adjust the throne to the right height for you.

Snare Drum Positioning

In jazz, the snare drum positioning is really vital. Because it's the best approach for me, I have played my snare drum at a straight position for many years, especially with the brushes and for the left hand to get an overall smoother sound on the instrument. It's ultimately up to you to find what works best for your personal technique.

Snare Drum Height

Next to the height of the drum throne, you must experiment with how high your snare drum is. Be careful; when you sit high and set your snare drum up low, it can cause tension in the back that creates more difficulty and even potential injuries.

Years ago, Lewis Nash gave me a piece of advice: "The top of your belt buckle should be parallel to the top rim of the snare drum." I have often used that as a guide to make sure I have the right height.

To Tilt or Not Tilt

"To tilt or not tilt, that is the question," that many great players have debated. The subject is a huge point of contention especially for jazz drummers of the modern generation. This is because so many of the great drummers of the previous generations of players—Kenny Washington, Lewis Nash, Jeff "Tain" Watts, Herlin Riley, Greg Hutchinson, Willie Jones III—tilt their snare drums while, generally speaking, my friends and I prefer not to tilt.

In fact, it definitely feels great to tilt the drum when I am playing traditional grip with sticks. However, for the versatility of brush playing, I find that having my drum flat/parallel works best for me.

Oddly enough, I was on tour years ago with Christian McBride, and we ran into Steve Gadd. It was then that I had a chance to speak with him at length about his drum setup. One of the questions I asked him was how he maintained his snare position given the fact that he is mostly a groove drummer. He told me he plays traditional grip going back to his early days of marching percussion. That was what contributed to his approach, and no matter the genre or styles he plays, his setup doesn't change.

Ultimately, I think you have to practice and see what works the best for you. Let sound and comfort be your guide.

CHAPTER 12: Brush Fills and Embellishments

The early brush players had a commitment to playing time.

By now, you know what I consider to be the golden rule of drumming: keep time. Yet it never fails that when I ask a student to play brushes, they most often can't even get past two bars of consistent time without a drum fill.

Many drummers have told me that after seeing video clips of my brush playing on YouTube, Instagram, Facebook, and during live performances, they begin to wonder about my choice of brush fills. They focus so much on brush fills that the time-keeping has no focus, direction, or stability. Brush fills should be an additive and enhancement, not the sole focus of your playing. There are multiple ways with the right hand and left hand to play light fills, but they should support your brush time-keeping, not get in the way of it.

The Vernel Fournier recordings with the Ahmad Jamal Trio completely altered my brush sound in terms of embellishments. I was kind of faking it a little bit, but when I began to study Vernel, my playing really came together. Vernel always played with great time, and his brush fills were smooth, tasteful, and musical.

On Count Basie and Oscar Peterson's recording *Satch and Josh... Again*, Louis Bellson plays a triplet fill that I love. I added it to my brush vocabulary, and it musically fits for so many things. Each of the following examples show the different fills that can be played either at midpoints or the end of your phrases:

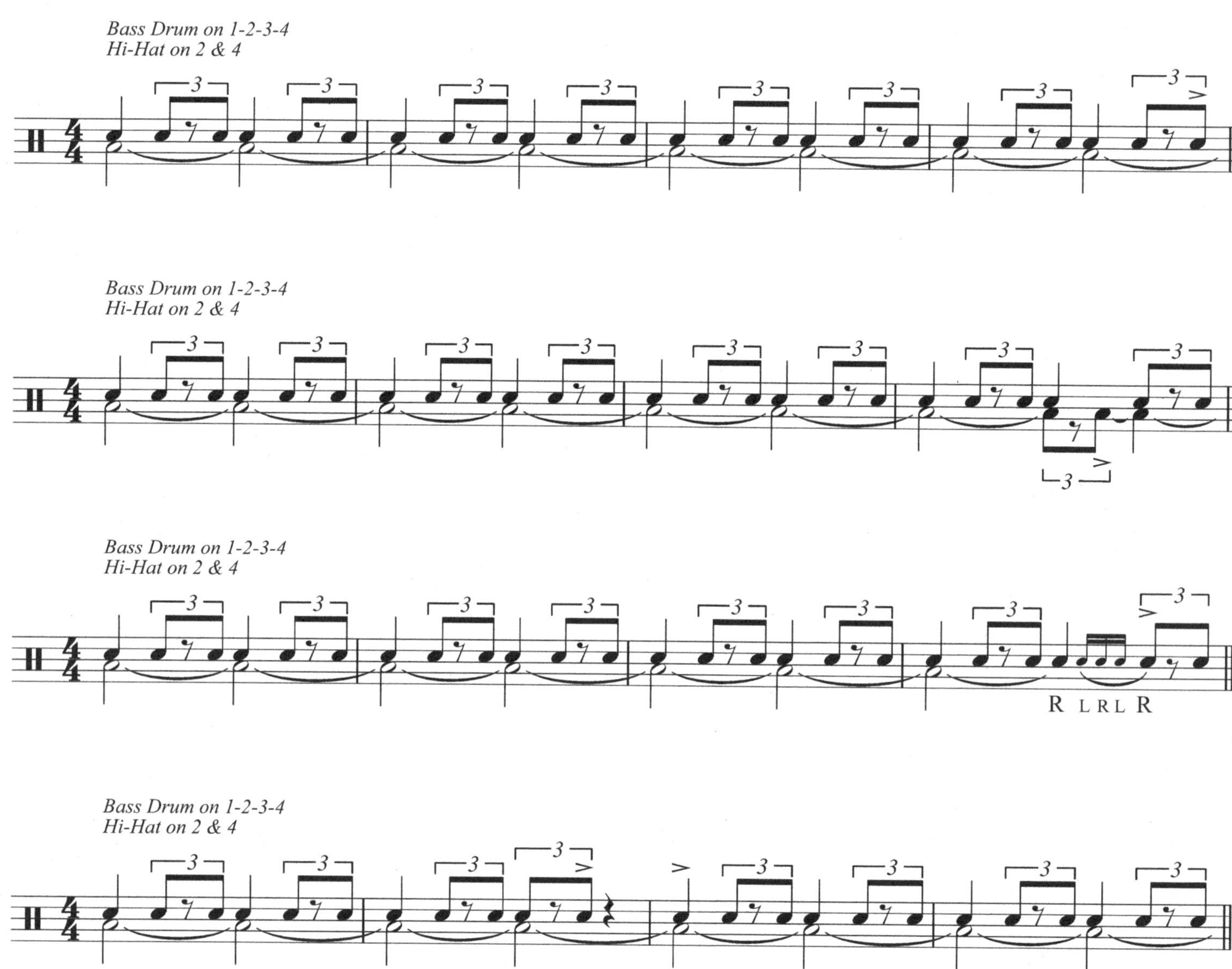

Brushes Around the Drums

Most of what you will learn in this book is how to effectively play time with the brushes on the snare drum. However, when soloing and playing various fills and enhancements, you can definitely apply these techniques to other parts of the drum kit. Nevertheless, my goal is to create a fundamental understanding of effective time-keeping.

Special Effects with Brushes

In the 1920s, drummers were already being creative with the brushes and finding multiple ways to play and orchestrate them within the music. There are a few parts of the brushes that have been instrumental in creating special effect sounds that are important in adding to the music.

Cymbal Choke

The cymbal choke involves the shaft of the brush being played with your right hand on the hi-hat with both cymbals half-open. Then with the left hand, you hold the hi-hat cymbals with pressure, and it creates the choking sound. You can also do this with the crash or ride cymbals, shown here in the following illustration:

Swinging with the Brush End

The brushes can be used in so many ways beyond only the wires. You can also utilize the end of the brushes to play the spang-a-lang pattern on the cymbal. Reference the same illustration of the cymbal choke to see how to use the end of the brush.

Swinging with the Brush Shaft

The part of the brush that is used while playing the choke cymbal sound is the same part that can be utilized to swing in the old school way, like a lot of the early jazz players.

A few exercises below will help you work this out:

1. Play time and accent on the "and" of beat 3.
2. Play time and accent on the "and" of beat 1 and the "and" of beat 3.
3. Play time for three bars and then play a drag fill to finish out a 4-bar phrase.

Sliding with the Brushes

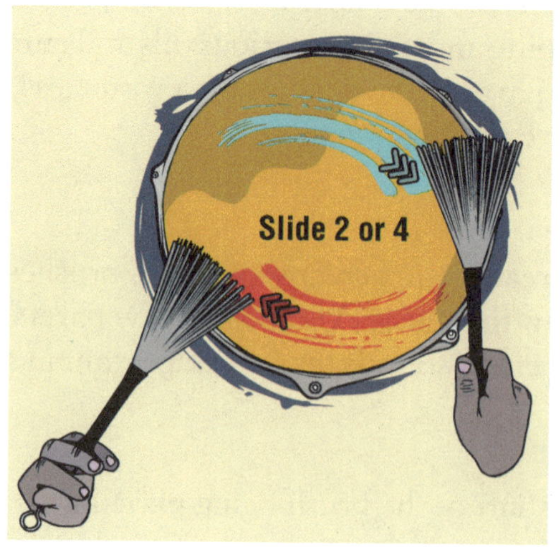

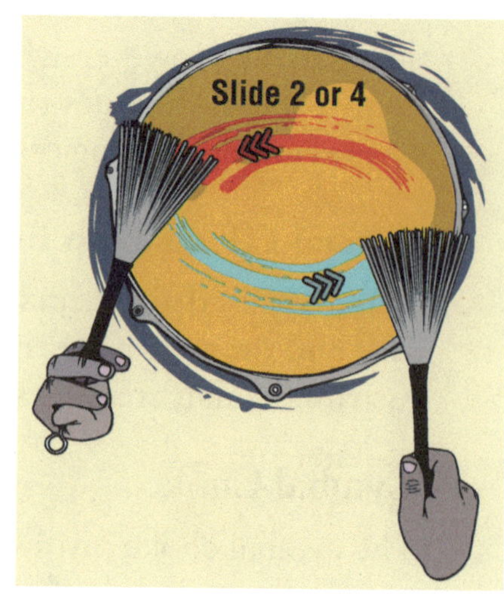

A key element with the brushes is sliding. A few exercises below can help you to establish your vocabulary:

1. Play quarter notes (unison) and slide on beat 4.

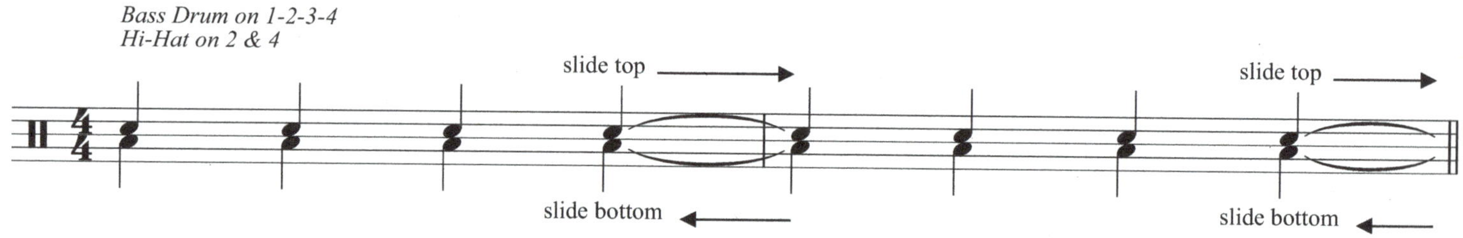

2. Play quarter notes (unison) and slide on beats 2 and 4.

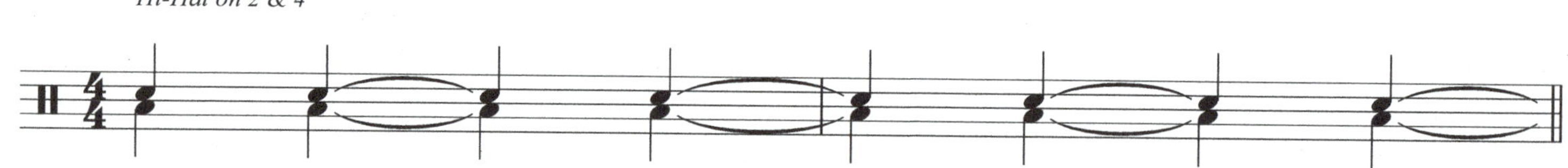

3. Play quarter notes (unison) and slide on beats 2 and 4 for one measure. Continue this in the next measure, but end with accenting on the "and" of beat 3.

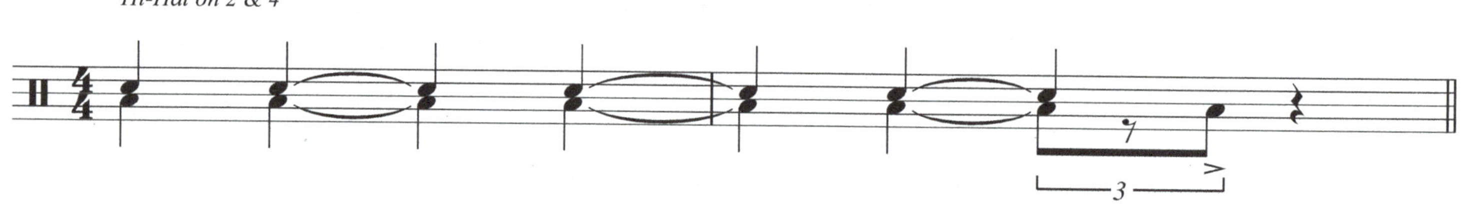

4. Play time for three bars and then play a drum fill beginning on the "and" of beat 1.

5. Play time for two bars and then slide on the "and" of beats 1 and 3.

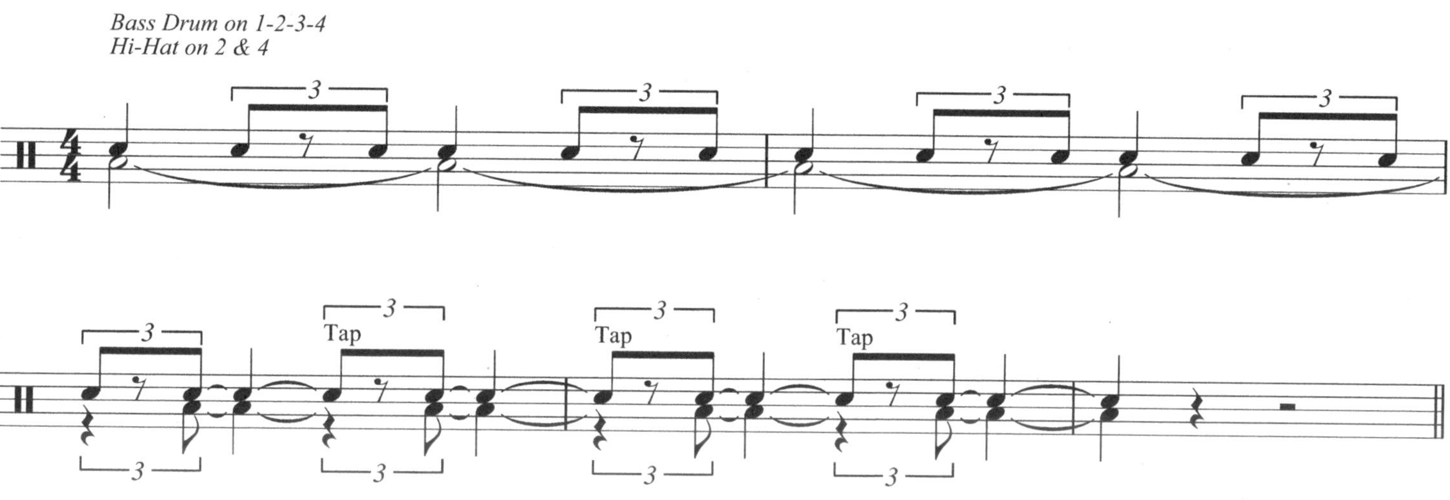

CHAPTER 13: Listen and Watch

One of the key habits that I have adapted since my early years of playing was the ability to self-analyze and be self-critical (within reason) for the sake of musical growth.

No matter how old we are or how long we've been at it, we are all always still evolving as drummers and musicians. I think the great Benny Golson said it best: "Ulysses, I never will consider myself perfect or having musically arrived because that means I'll have to give it all up, and I don't plan on doing that soon."

I take these words to heart. We should not strive to be perfect as much as to constantly evolve as we learn to study and admire the masters and phenoms that play our instruments. As you learn, begin to constantly self-correct your own performance and critically assess the blocks between where you are and where you desire to be within your playing.

Listen to Your Playing

I often listen to recordings of my playing. Before I was fortunate enough to be in the studio as much as I am now, I would record myself on whatever I could: tape cassettes, mini-disc players, and Zoom recorders. My goal isn't to listen to what is working; rather, it is to listen to what *needs* work and what hasn't come together in my playing.

For instance, one of the questions I get often about my playing is the grip I use in my right hand (I play really far back on the stick). The way that came about was actually by me listening to my ride cymbal pattern. I noticed that I was rushing the spang-a-lang pattern, so I began to move my hand back on the stick and record about four bars of time.

When I listened back to the beat I liked, I settled on that position, and it's the one that I use currently. This may sound like something very miniscule, but I find that the great players in music take a detailed look at their technique over and over to honestly measure what is working and not working.

My advice to you is: Record four bars of yourself playing brushes, and then listen critically to what is and isn't working with a follow-up of fixing it. If you don't have it within your own knowledge and arsenal to fix it, then look closer at some of the areas I've recommended so far: Are you breathing? How's your posture? Is your throne a comfortable height? Are the wires on your snare the proper length for what you're trying to achieve? Are you keeping time? For so many difficulties at the drumset, a keen student can help him or herself with the right knowledge and tools. Should this still not be enough, then go to a professional teacher and ask for their assistance.

Watch Your Playing

When I first started studying with Carl Allen and Lewis Nash, the first thing they did was buy a full-length mirror and put it inside of the practice studio. It was one of the most dynamic teaching practices they could have done for me, simply because it made me watch myself while playing. Drums are very physical instruments, and it's important to understand that if it feels right, then it will look right, and therefore, most likely be right.

Carl Allen

It may seem banal, but purchasing a mirror to watch yourself practice can be a really helpful thing as you work to become a successful brush player. If possible, also visually record yourself playing the brushes, and then critique what you see. Watch every nuance of your body and breathing and how it affects your playing.

Record Your Playing

These days, people are handy with recording themselves, and it is a good habit to get into while you practice. I suggest students make a regular habit of recording their playing by capturing the best sound and visual quality they can for a fair self-critique. Those who do this will be much better prepared when it comes time to cut an album or create other content because they will have learned to listen critically to their own work. It is not always easy, but it is crucial to accept where you currently are in your musical development. If you are not where you want to be, then keep going. Keep going and... keep time.

Sound Is Key

When I was younger, I had the privilege of Kenny Washington always passionately yelling at me to say, "You've got to play the drums, kid!" That was something Papa Jo Jones would say to him. And when I asked him, "What do you mean Kenny?" he replied, "You've got to get inside of the instrument and bring sound out of the drum."

When I started studying with him, that's when I altered my brush technique to playing in the center of the drum so that I could really get a deep sound. Even though the recording quality varies, when I study the sound of Papa Jo and all the great masters of this art form, they just sound so good. Sound is key to me, and it's truly the evidence of an understanding of the art form and music.

PART 3: The Application

CHAPTER 14: Tools of the Trade

Now that we have discussed where brushes fit within musical history, I hope you have a better understanding of the musical concepts that are behind brush techniques and methods both past and present. We've covered some of the many nuances brushes can provide in grip, height, width, type of drumhead, use of accessories, and the attention to your body and breathing while playing. Now we can move on to something more on the practical side, yet crucial to get right for your own situation: my current drum setup for those that are looking for options within their own.

Brushes

Vic Firth Heritage Brush: I currently use and enjoy the consistency of this brush. Every pair I use feels the same, and I can rely on this brush to execute musical and technical ideas that I'm required to play.

I advise that you need to make sure that when you are practicing that the brush model you are using doesn't technically get in your way. Some brushes are constructed to be very big, and others are quite heavy, particularly the handle and the brush wires themselves. Try a few different types before choosing one exclusive brand or model.

Drumheads

Remo Coated Ambassador: I have been a fan and supporter of Remo Drumheads since I was incredibly young, and I was introduced to the coated Ambassador drumhead early in my jazz drum education. A popular choice among many players, it has been the sound for many great jazz drummers for decades. There are other companies that make similar drumheads, but they are mostly attempted replicas of this particular drumhead.

Drums

Tama Star Series: I have been a fan of Tama drums for many years. These drums are hand-manufactured in Japan by wonderful craftsmen that I have personally met. Their level of ingenuity and attention to every nut, bolt, and screw on the drum is second to none.

Drum Hardware

Tama Classic Hardware: Another key element to effectively playing the brushes is the type of materials that makes up the snare drum, bass drum, toms, and even the drum throne you are sitting on, and how those pieces of hardware are constructed. Tama is a dynamic and rare company that makes great drums and wonderful hardware. I have been using cymbal stands, snare drum stands, foot pedals, and hi-hat stands that are part of the Tama Classic Hardware series, which was designed by drummer Peter Erskine and the Tama Drum technicians. They figured out how to replicate some of the older single, flat-base vintage jazz drum hardware, updating it to be more dependable and sturdy. Tama also has multiple drum throne models that are really supportive and aid in great posture and balance on the kit.

Good Gear vs. Great Gear

It is important to say here that not every drummer is rich, and many drummers aren't able to purchase expensive drums and hardware when first getting started. I was told many years ago that Papa Jo Jones used to walk around New York City with a newspaper under his arm, and whenever he took it out, there were a pair of brushes inside. He would lay that newspaper on a counter or flat surface, and he would play some of the most amazing time with brushes for all who were there to listen and watch him.

It's great to have good gear, but it is not the determining factor in getting better at this art form. You are the key ingredient to sounding better. It has taken years for me to have the right gear, and this is not unusual even for the best drummers. But what is important for *all* drummers is the right pair of brushes and a drumhead that you can practice with. Attain those two tools and then work on perfecting your technique.

CHAPTER 15: Performance Scenarios with Brushes

In the next chapter, I will discuss the different ways that you can use the brushes in various scenarios and how to play more effectively within them.

Brushes with a Rhythm Section

One of the most important roles of the drummer is to firstly connect with the rhythm section, which is the foundation of most music. Many young drummers fail to understand how to play to maintain their presence and achieve a full sound with the brushes. It's still important to keep the connection with the bass player just as you would with sticks and the ride cymbal.

When I first learned to play the swing pattern with the drumsticks, I was taught a role for each hand and limb, learning how they were directly connected to a role that a rhythm section member would play as well.

> **Right Hand/Ride Cymbal:** The spang-a-lang pattern that I have referred to frequently is to be played in the right hand, and the goal is to connect the quarter notes within that pattern to the upright bass. My aim is to connect my beat to every part of the bass player's beat so that we can form a united groove, creating a foundation for the ensemble.
>
> **Left Foot/Hi-Hat:** My target is to play beats 2 and 4 on the hi-hat and connect that to the upright bass as well. This is important in helping the horn players, vocalists, and the rest of the rhythm section feel the swing groove and to always know where they are within the beat.
>
> **Left Hand:** When playing with drumsticks, you use the left hand to play comping rhythms. This hand is also supposed to lock up with the left hand of the pianist and their rhythms. When playing the brushes, it's a similar connection; you just have to balance your comping rhythms with the stirring/sweeping as well.
>
> **Right Foot:** Some drummers believe in feathering the bass drum, and others don't. I believe in knowing how to do it so that you always have the option to play it or not. I lock up my right foot with the upright bass, feathering softly. If I desire to interact with the soloist, then the bass drum is a great tool for me to connect with the horn player along with the rest of the rhythm section.

It's important as a drummer to understand which limb is connected to the various roles of the rhythm section and other surrounding members in the ensemble. It's crucial to fully understand and play with that responsibility in mind.

Brushes with a Vocalist

The initial way that I started to refine my brush playing was with vocalists because half of their repertoire required me to play ballads. These ballads include slow, medium, and uptempo songs, and I still had to figure out how to be musical while playing with the vocalists who sang them.

The first gig I remember that tested my brush playing was in New York City when the National Jazz Museum in Harlem had just opened. I was invited by Loren Schoenberg to play with the late legendary singer Milt Grayson for an event. I was playing time with the brushes, but Mr. Grayson could not feel my time as strong as he desired, so he looked over at me and asked me to play the hi-hat louder. I was so embarrassed, but it made me go home and shed on learning how to sound strong and cohesive without the hi-hat.

Playing with a vocalist is largely about learning how to be subtle and tasty with fills in addition to having a command on multiple styles to play. I find that when you look at a set list with a jazz vocalist and see that 60–70 percent of the tunes involve playing brushes, you need to begin looking for new ways to play tunes. Stop playing the traditional pattern on the snare drum only, and begin to learn how to orchestrate your playing on the other parts of the drumset.

I feel that playing with so many vocalists has really helped me to shape the musical side of my brush playing and all-around performance. I would advise every student to seek the opportunity to develop more skills in this area as well.

Brushes with a Small Ensemble (Trio, Quartet, Quintet)

Most drummers are constantly figuring out ways to play brushes beyond the confines of the rhythm section, especially within small ensembles that include horns.

As we've discussed, the first issue is maintaining the appropriate volume and fullness of sound that can sustain and support the ensemble, which requires a serious grasp of technique.

Your goal should be to stay in tune with the roles that you need to play as a drummer, even while playing the brushes. You must realize that the more the ensemble expands, the deeper your groove should become as you choose how to respond musically to the other parts being played.

Sometimes I find that when a horn player gets on the bandstand, drummers almost become musical parakeets, repeating every rhythm played by the horns to prove they are really interacting. When this happens and a drummer is playing brushes, the time can become very congested and difficult for the horn player to have clarity and space to create unhindered.

It's here again that we can keep faith with the drummer's golden rule: keep time. If you are playing your brushes with a trio, quintet, sextet, or any other ensemble, then play solid time, and the band will love you!

Brushes with a Big Band

Some of my favorite drummers, like Mel Lewis, Sonny Payne, Herlin Riley, and many others, have mastered how to play the brushes within the context of a big band. What they do is particularly challenging, but it's just the same technique that has already been discussed and demonstrated. If perfected, then it will allow you to propel a big band with the brushes.

Again, it is all about learning how to get a deeper sound from the center of the drums and utilizing the feathering of the bass drum. Those techniques are what will give the big band more of a pulse to hold onto while playing the brushes. This takes a lot of practice. For instance, when playing a big band chart, you don't want to have the bottom drop all of a sudden in the band when the passage with the brushes comes up.

Confidence is key within the big band when playing with brushes or sticks. If you don't carry that confidence, then the band will, as they say, smell your nervous energy and possibly start hurling orders and demands at you.

I remember the first time I got called to play with the Count Basie Orchestra. We started playing the famous "Shiny Stockings" piece. All the jazz aficionados and drummers know this piece has a huge "shout" section with a drum feature, and it is a classic piece within big band repertoire. However, I was about 26 years old and not fully confident in my sound yet. That band played one tempo, and I was playing another, which prompted them to look at me and start laughing. My friend pulled me aside and said, "Man, this band has been playing one way for many years, so you need to pull it together." So I went deep within myself and found that confidence. We had a great time together, so much that they asked me to join the band after that tour!

CHAPTER 16: Recording with the Brushes

There is a famous story that Tommy Rockwell, the man who produced many of Louis Armstrong's early jazz recordings, literally had to hold Zutty Singleton's snare drum over the microphone while he stood playing on the track "Muggles." It was in the early days of brushes and recording, and it was incredibly difficult to capture the sound.

Thankfully, we don't have to do that anymore. There are many great microphones that can properly capture the sound of the brushes. Much of the recording of the brushes has to do with microphone placement, which usually involves working with an engineer who understands the sound of the brushes. The engineer can choose the right microphone to capture the precise sound being played by the drummer.

One of the first recordings of the brushes that truly gave me something to aspire for was when I started researching Kenny Washington before becoming one of his personal students. There is a recording from the Criss Cross label featuring an early version of the Bill Charlap Trio on a tune called "All Through the Night." On that composition, Kenny is beautifully keeping time and orchestrating the brushes around the kit. It's captured perfectly.

On the play-along recordings for this book, my engineer Chris and I used two microphones on the snare drum because I wanted to make sure that we captured the fullness of the brush sound so you can hear my sound clearly.

Direct Mics

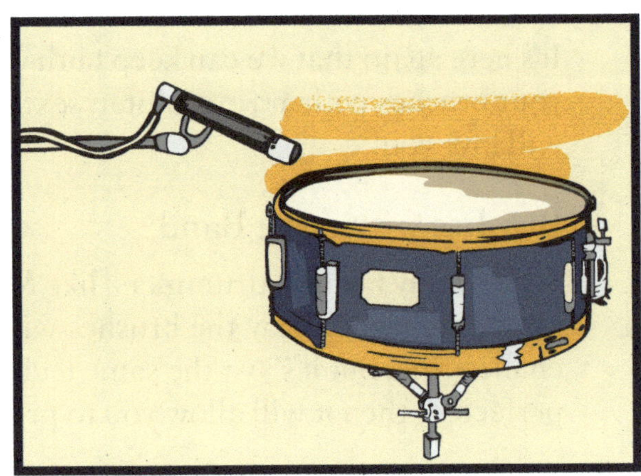

David Darlington is a Grammy award-winning recording and mixing engineer who I've been fortunate enough to work with for close to a decade as a producer and artist. After the many records we have worked on together, I now understand the importance of the quality of the microphone and how you place it when recording a vocalist or instruments. The placement is crucial, but you also need to understand the pattern and phasing of the microphone in addition to the direction of how it picks up sound and records. David and I worked together on a list of microphones that we like to use for recording:

Shure SM57: This a dynamic mic that captures a lot of detail and can take a lot of sound pressure level (SPL). You will need to adjust the equalization (EQ) for brushes.

AKG 414: There are lots of details in this large condenser. It has a great high end, and the hypercardioid[4] pattern rejects the hi-hat and overheads to focus on the snare.

Neumann KM 84: This is a very bright, small condenser that accurately captures the brushes with great detail.

Sennheiser 441: This is another dynamic mic that always sounds great on the snare.

4 "Polar pattern used to describe microphone pick up characteristics… with the primary sensitivity in front of the microphone… but has less sensitivity at [its] sides and only slightly more directly behind."–Sweetwater.com

Live Sound

A few years ago, I started traveling with my own microphones on the road when I began touring with Kurt Elling and Christian McBride. Kurt and Christian always had their own microphones, and they hired road managers and sound engineers who could create a consistent sound on the road no matter which venue.

When I saw how serious they were about their sound, I started investigating what the best microphones were for me to utilize on the drums given my particular sound and technique. I immediately thought about my brush playing, and I found a great set of microphones from the company Earthworks. These are supercardioid[5] microphones that excellently capture the articulate details of my sound, especially when playing brushes. To be more specific, I prefer the **Earthworks SR30** and **TC25** overhead microphones.

5 "Polar pattern... similar to, and often confused with, the hypercardioid pattern... slightly less directional [with] a smaller lobe of sensitivity."—Sweetwater.com

PART 4: Recording and Play-Along

CHAPTER 17: Keys to Playing Good Time

One of the key aspects of learning to play good time with brushes is to play with other musicians as much as you can. If you aren't able to play along with musicians in the same room, then you can play along with master musicians via recordings.

Like many other aspiring young musicians, I began to improve my time-playing by sitting in my room playing along with recordings. As one mentor told me years ago, "You may never get to play with Ray Brown, Ron Carter, and many of the great bass players, but you can if you play and practice with their records."

Coming up, I always searched to find recordings of great piano trios—Oscar Peterson, Ahmad Jamal, Ray Bryant—but when I started studying with Kenny Washington, he gave me a disc of some wonderful drummer-less recordings and instructed me to learn the arrangements. This assignment completely added another level to my playing. It taught me about orchestration, space, time, musicality, and so many other wonderful lessons.

Following this thought, I want you to hone in on playing with the tracks explained in the next few chapters. Seek to orchestrate and create your own drum parts on the tracks without drums. Don't forget to have fun with it, and don't forget to breathe!

What to Listen For

There are three key things to listen for when playing along with recordings:

1. As a drummer, the first thing I listen for when playing with a recording or live is the bass player. I listen first to the pulse of the bass, and I make sure to lock up with that. The left hand of the brushes should be treated like the hi-hat (beats 2 and 4) locking in with the pulse of the bass. The right hand of the brushes should be treated like the spang-a-lang ride cymbal pattern and lock in with the walking bass line as well.
2. The second thing to listen for is the harmony being played by the chordal instruments (piano or guitar) so you can understand the harmonic form of the piece. This will help establish if you are playing a blues (12-bar) form, rhythm changes form, AABA, etc.
3. Thirdly, listen and make sure that your time-keeping is informed by the melody. I always say that "melody is king." Each drummer should be able to sing the melody to any song they are playing to allow them to make the right decisions while keeping time in a way that is musical. It's not just about the technique.

CHAPTER 18: The Trio and Voice

I feel it is important for all of my students to have an example of how to play along with the music and arrangements, and I find it helpful to let them study from one of my own performances on certain tracks.

Playing with a recorded track can be an awesome learning experience when done with intention, so take advantage of the opportunity to play with a stellar trio of strong musicians. Practice with these recordings as much as you can. On the tracks that come with this book, I made a point to utilize realistic musical forms and scenarios that you will encounter on the bandstand. You can approach and transcribe what I have played, and you can also begin to create your own drum parts as you become more comfortable with the tracks.

I also wanted to create a portion of the recording with the drums removed so that you can practice on your own with a track; be sure to learn the arrangements so that you can musically become part of the ensemble. You'll hear me do it, but then it'll be your turn. As I would do, be mindful of your body and breath. Don't just play "at" the recording; play *with* the recording as if you are a part of the ensemble.

Trio Tracks with Drums

Track 1

Track 1 w/o drums

"My Sweetheart" (Ballad)**:** This is a basic ballad, and my goal was to play really solid time so that all of you can have an example of how to play basic time on a ballad when playing along with the drum-less track.

Track 2

Track 2 w/o drums

"Skip Trace" (Uptempo Swing)**:** This is a fun tune that Mike King and I created to have some fun with. It is definitely a brisk tempo, but check it out anyway. I played in a more soloistic nature and used a lot of embellishments on this tune. However, even with the embellishments, you'll notice I am still bowing to my golden rule by keeping time as my first priority. Try to keep this in mind when you are playing with just the piano and bass.

Track 3

Track 3 w/o drums

"Someday" (Waltz in 3/4)**:** This tune is based on "Someday My Prince Will Come," but in a minor key with some harmonic alterations. My goal was to utilize the 3/4 waltz pattern, but also play at times with a more "floaty" feel to match the vibe of the tune.

When you play to this track with just the piano and bass, try to stay true to the pattern that I provided. However, you can use your own version of a 3/4 pattern with the brushes as long as it blends well with the ensemble.

Track 4

Track 4 w/o drums

"Truth" (Medium Swing)**:** This tune is based on Thelonious Monk's tune "Evidence," which itself is a **contrafact** (new melody based on existing chord changes) of "Just You, Just Me" by Jesse Greer and Raymond Klages, and it plays a lot with syncopation. My goal on this tune was not to overplay in the spaces but to use them as a tool to be musical. Pay attention; you can hear that at times, I try to really set up the hits for the rhythm section. Try to emulate the same approach when playing along with only piano and bass.

Track 5

Track 5 w/o drums

"Gregory's N'Awlins Strut" (Medium)**:** In this tune written by my good friend Liston Gregory III (he and Michael King are featured on this track), I hope to channel O'Neil Spencer, Andrew Hilaire, and all of the wonderful early jazz drummers. My goal is to give you an example of the beautiful simplicity and taste in their keeping of time.

When playing along with only piano and bass, I want you to reference the early jazz examples that we looked at earlier, sticking to quarter-note and eighth-note patterns. Don't use the spang-a-lang pattern, which technically hadn't existed yet.

Track 6

Track 6 w/o drums

"Gregory's N'Awlins Strut" (Uptempo)**:** Again, my goal here is to continue channeling the great early drummers while keeping it steady. It's crucial to make sure the fast tempo doesn't sound frantic. To play simple time that fast can be a challenge even for experienced drummers. Have fun and try to keep the groove really focused and together when you play along with just the piano and bass.

Vocal Tracks with Drums

Track 7

Track 7 w/o drums

"Karlea's Bop": As I've discussed, one of my favorite things as a drummer is to play with singers. This track was one I had the pleasure to record with Karlea Lynné. Working with Karlea is a dream because she is really rhythmic, she listens, and she has a great sense of time. This tune of hers was a chance to showcase that particular part of her nuanced musicality. She and I begin the tune together, and the intention for me, as the drummer, is to be active with her rhythmically but not get in her way. You can hear how we trade phrases as a band during the solo section. See if you can follow where we really tried to feed off each other's ideas.

When you play along with just the piano and bass, try to interact with Karlea in a similar way that I did. You can also play just as much as you can, practicing in phrases until you learn the entire song.

Track 8

Track 8 w/o drums

"Innocence of a Child": This is a beautiful ballad that Karlea wrote the lyrics to. My goal was not to only accompany her with the ballad brush pattern, but to play musically in a manner that complimented her while supporting the rhythm section. Try to sound like "the ocean" and hear yourself as part of the ensemble when you play with just the piano and bass.

Track 9

Track 9 w/o drums

"Missing Mr. Blues": I always love playing the blues! But I normally play the blues with drumsticks, usually leading with the ride cymbal. On this track, I take the opportunity to still provide that same pulse but with brushes. I challenge you to play the strong swing feel as I did when you play along with just piano and bass!

Track 10

Track 10 w/o drums

"Where the Dawn Goes": This tune is based on "How High the Moon." Matt and I chose to play a two-feel on the A section of the tune, so we really made sure to create a difference in the time-feel while not disturbing the melody, and again, keeping things solid for the vocalist and the rhythm section. It's important that the bass player and drummer are in agreement when they change the time-feel. Sometimes it's cool to have a quick conversation before playing to make sure everyone is musically on the same page.

When you play with only the piano and bass, try to lock in with the bass on the two-feel while supporting Karlea, taking care to nail the transitions from the two-feel to the regular 4/4 groove.

Bass Duo with Drums

Track 11

Track 11 w/o drums

"Blues" (Medium Tempo)**:** We'll do a few passes with the hi-hat on beats 2 and 4 and then additional ones without the hi-hat. The last few choruses will feature both the left and right hands playing unaccented throughout the form.

Track 12

Track 12 w/o drums

"Blues" (Uptempo)**:** Be sure to lock your right hand with the bass player. Play the first few choruses with the hi-hat on beats 2 and 4, and then on the next few choruses, have only the left hand accent those beats. The final choruses should be played with no accented beats.

Track 13

Track 13 w/o drums

"Rhythm Changes": Follow the same format in the blues tracks with the first chorus featuring the hi-hat on beats 2 and 4, the second chorus with no hi-hat, and the third chorus with no accented beats.

Track 14

Track 14 w/o drums

"Two-Feel": On the last few choruses, change your left-hand sweeping pattern to counterclockwise. There is a noticeable difference in the sound.

PART 5: Video Display of Technique

CHAPTER 19: The Metronome

The metronome in my opinion is God's gift to the drummer. Of course, if keeping good time is a problem for you, then I suppose it could be your enemy. Regardless, every musician must practice with a metronome sometimes because ultimately, your time has to stay in line with the metronome like everybody else's. When you practice with the metronome, choose varying tempos to work with so that you have versatility in your time-keeping and tempo choices. We denote the speed of the metronome by beats per minute (bpm).

Patterns

This portion of the book features explanations of the patterns in the instructional videos and audio, where I show you how to properly work through each pattern and address the challenges that are presented.

Video 1

Track 15

Uptempo

I actually like to play with the metronome set to the half note. Set your metronome to 180 bpm and alternate between regular and double-time playing.

Video 2

Track 16

Ballad

Always be sure to fully concentrate on keeping time when playing ballads. It's easy to lose track of your time-keeping when playing in this style, but it's crucial to set the foundation for the band. The hi-hat is optional in this style of playing as the left hand can be used to accent beats 2 and 4.

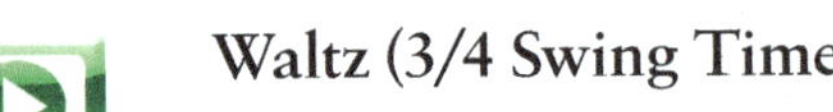
Video 3

Track 17

Waltz (3/4 Swing Time)

Playing a waltz can be difficult if you're used to only playing in 4/4 time. The accented beats usually fall on beats 2 and 3, and you can use either the hi-hat or the left hand to emphasize those beats.

Video 4

Track 18

Clockwise

In this exercise, feather the bass drum on each beat and play the hi-hat with the foot on beats 2 and 4. Use your left hand to sweep, accenting along with the hi-hat. The right hand should mimic the same consistency with which you play the ride cymbal.

Try switching to double-time playing after you initially master this technique at the regular tempo.

Video 5

Track 19

Counterclockwise

Build this pattern from the ground up just as we did with the clockwise brush pattern. It will follow the same procedure as the previous exercises, but the motion of the left hand travels in the opposite direction. Switch back and forth between a moderate tempo and double-time playing.

Special Effects

The unique physical nature of the brushes gives us opportunities to use some special effects such as deadstrokes (notated with a [+] sign) and sliding. Both are signature to the brushes, and they are key components to expanding your brush vocabulary in both time-keeping and soloing.

Swinging with Rudiments

An easy way to build solo vocabulary for drummers is to use rudiments, adding swing phrasing to them. Using the rudiments creatively with the jazz phrasing can add so much vocabulary for you to use within a song for comping or soloing.

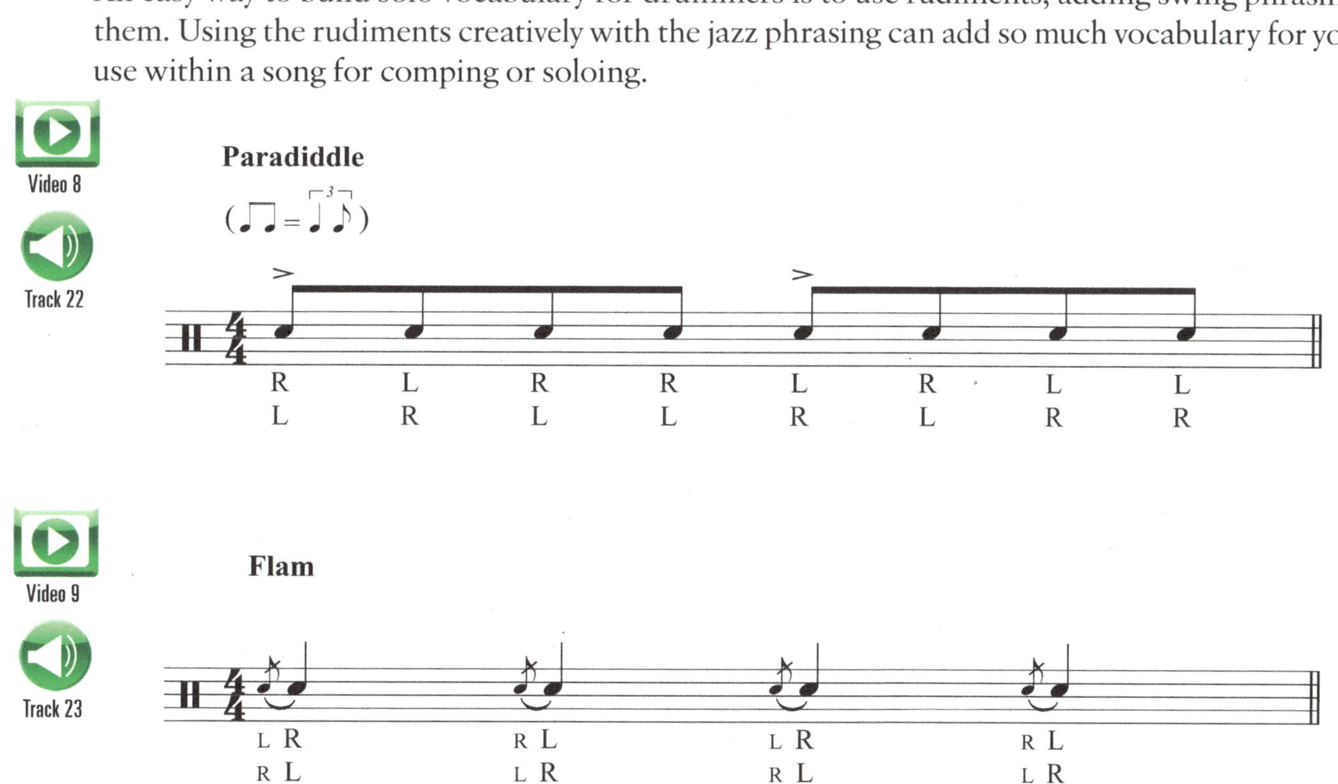

CHAPTER 20: Trading Phrases and Coaching a Student

Trading two bars, four bars, or eight bars is a standard yet unique element to jazz music. Particularly when soloing with drums, often times another musician will choose to "trade" with you, going back and forth with your soloing. When a trade happens, you must keep your soloing in perfect time so that it does not disrupt the musical form.

On this track, you will first hear me play time for four bars and then solo. The same format will be applied to trading between playing time and soloing, first over two bars and then eight bars.

Solo Trading

Video 10

Track 24

1. Trading fours with Ulysses
2. Trading twos with Ulysses
3. Trading eights with Ulysses

Coaching with Aaron Jennings

Much of the same information that we've discussed so far is what I addressed in a lesson that I recorded with a former student of mine, Aaron Jennings:

Video 11

Coaching Aaron, Clockwise

Video 12

Coaching Aaron, Counterclockwise

Video 13

Coaching Aaron, Waltz

Video 14

Coaching Aaron, Uptempo

Bonus Interview with Aaron Jennings

Video 15

Track 25

I had a chat with my student about questions he had concerning the brushes in addition to being a young student on the rise in New York City studying jazz in 2019.

PART 6: Perfecting the Gift

CHAPTER 21: The Importance of Practice

So far, the contents of this book, along with the audio tracks, listening, video, and play-along instruction, should make you feel as if you have some tools for effective practicing. It is not just sitting down at the kit and taking a swing. You want to get your body and breathing right, throne in the correct placement, and grip of the brush where you need it. Practice with the snare on and then off. Spend part of your practice routine using the metronome, then without it, and then with it going twice as fast as before. Practice with vocalists; play along with tracks where you can hear the drums or where you must become the drummer yourself. However you practice, just do it a lot!

Earlier in the book, I mentioned a YouTube clip of me playing brushes at a very fast tempo with the Christian McBride Trio—a clip that has become really popular amongst young drummers. Whenever I travel or do panels, the first question is often something along the lines of, "How did you learn how to play brushes at such a blistering tempo and make it look so easy?" I tell them, "What you learn to effectively play slow, you can play fast. But in order to do that, you need to practice playing fast. And in order to make it look easy, you've got to practice playing fast *a lot*." The expression "practice makes perfect" exists for a reason. There is no secret to getting better at something; you just have to practice, practice, practice, and then do it some more!

In his terrific book *Outliers*, Malcolm Gladwell—one of the great minds of our time—writes about the "10,000 hour rule." This simple concept poses that, at least in theory, anyone can become a superlative master of any artistic or athletic form if they just accrue 10,000 hours in practice and experience. Whether you complete these hours in 20 hours a week over 10 years, 10 hours a week in 20 years, or any other variable with that, Gladwell's point is that anyone can be a master if they just practice enough.

Twenty hours a week for 10 years sounds like a long haul, but for many musicians, your passion for the music starts so young that you get a nice early start. From the time I was about three or four years of age, I loved to practice the drums so much that when my parents needed me to improve in school, they didn't restrict my outside television time. They knew exactly how to get me: they would take away my drums. As I watched with inner agony, my drum kit would be whisked away to some faraway place. Some people reading this may say that it sounds cruel, but my folks knew what they were doing. I would have done anything to get my drums back. Within weeks, my grades would improve, and my precious drums would be back in my room.

When it came to the drums, no one ever had to make me practice. From my earliest memories, I have loved music so dearly, and I have always been compelled to get better at my craft, even as a child. Growing up, if I could have practiced 20 hours a week, then I would have. Sometimes I'm sure I came close, which just shows you that sometimes you can be well on your way to "10,000 hours" before you know it.

Practice Is a Mindset

There are multiple ways to practice, but for me, the first is mental practicing. I usually take a piece of music and listen to it with headphones, allowing my mind to fully comprehend the concept and piece. Before I ever sit down at my drum kit, I attack the piece intellectually: What sort of mental blocks do I need to work through? What kind of physicality do I need to achieve? What is my comprehension level of this particular piece? I listen to the melody, form, and harmonic structure to digest the piece and get it ingrained into my mind before touching the drums.

The same goes for the brushes: you have to spend time hearing the sound in your mind in order to make your hands and limbs physically figure out how to accomplish the sound that you hear in your mind's ear.

I believe in having and maintaining a musical imagination. In saying that, I suggest that you, too, get accustomed to imagining yourself playing at the highest level. As a brush player, I always imagine my brushes sounding crisp, balanced, and grooving in a way that truly supports any artist I work with.

Tools Necessary for the Shed

We've talked generally about many of the tools you will need in your practice room, or "shed" as we musicians sometimes call it. It's helpful to have an adequate drum kit, especially a snare drum, along with a metronome, small speakers, and a mirror. You can vary this setup depending on what you have access to, but the basic ingredients are there.

Drum Kit: You are a drummer; you know why you need this!

Snare Drum: Occasionally separate your snare drum from the kit, and practice with it so that you don't have the limbs as a distraction in your development. Certain things need to be adhered to when pertaining to the hands.

Metronome: How can we as drummers have good time-keeping skills if we never check in with the perfect time of the metronome? Did you know it's true that every human being has an internal clock and tempo metric? Depending on the kind of music I am playing most often at the time, I find my internal clock will adjust to that tempo. For instance, if I am playing a lot of straight-ahead jazz music, I will naturally hear the time incredibly on top of the beat. If I have been playing funk music or in church, I'll hear the time more in the center of the beat. Checking in with the metronome allows me to check my internal clock with what we consider the perfect time and then re-align my inner tempo. Trust me, no matter how experienced you are, every player needs to check in with true time every once in a while. Keeping good time is one aspect of our music that we must practice as we do all our other talents.

Mirror: As I mentioned earlier, it was Carl Allen and Lewis Nash who I first saw put a mirror in the studio, and I've done it ever since. A drummer needs to watch their movements to really understand their performance like a dancer or athlete. You need to regularly practice with a mirror in the room so you can watch your form, posture, and technique in order to be truly aware of what you are doing physically.

Small Speakers: I know some people who go out and buy the fanciest sound system they can find to put in their shed. Top-of-the-line speakers are helpful for listening to music because they will allow you to hear more of what is happening in the music. However, for our purposes here, I think it is really important to have a set of small desktop speakers. I use mine to listen to recordings and play along with the brushes. Some of my students do this in their lessons, and they ask me to turn the music up, to which I say, "No." The goal is to play dynamically, adjusting your dynamic level and volume to the sound of the speakers in addition to helping find balance with an ensemble or vocalist. This is especially valuable in the long-term when you work on your touch and ability to adjust to the various venues in which you will perform with different artists.

Practice in the Shed

Once you have the desired sound of the brushes in your head, then sit down in the shed and work it out physically.

Sit in front of the snare drum away from the drum kit. Making sure your posture is correct, alternate playing with some records and with the metronome until the sound is right. Remember: you have to be self-critical and analyze what is not working with your technique.

Practice on the Job

When we first started playing "Cherokee" with McBride, I have to humbly admit that I was struggling with the tempo initially. But McBride always had a habit of forcing you to play something difficult night after night until it became a joy with ease. So essentially, all of us were practicing on the job, and it was great every night figuring out how to work out my weaknesses and turn them into strengths.

It is possible to have a gig and constantly work things out in the midst of the opportunity, but obviously use this advice with extreme caution. I am not saying to show up unprepared, but use your opportunities to practice on the job with discretion. In the beginning when we would play "Cherokee," we could still get through the tune pretty well, and much of the struggling was only noticeable to us internally as a trio.

Everyone has heard the joke of the tourist asking, "Excuse me, how do you get to Carnegie Hall?" and the guy answers, "PRACTICE!" I'm sure someone is going to ask, "Well, what about when you are at Carnegie Hall, are you practicing?" Not necessarily, but I also believe that every day that I play the drums is a day I am getting better and more familiar with my craft. The time I have spent playing in real musical situations where there is an audience is the best possible kind of practice because it forces you to work on practicality and artistry.

Practice with Others

I am definitely a proponent of isolated practice for many reasons but primarily because musicians are all on different levels of proficiency. There are certain things that have to be accomplished personally before you are able to have a great collective collaboration with other musicians.

However, that does not mean you should only practice alone. As a drummer, I am a big proponent of practicing with the rhythm section, vocalists, and others. So much of our playing with the brushes and the drum kit as a whole will improve in the context of practicing with other people.

Be Intentional and Consistent with Practicing

It's important to be intentional within your practice routine; otherwise, it will be very difficult to guarantee results within your playing. I believe in setting goals before you start your practice time, and make sure that you structure your time wisely around achieving those goals. Intentionality is about having a specific goal and result in mind from the beginning of your pursuits and designing an efficient plan to achieve that intention. Maintain a consistency of focus with your goals, and don't change what you are working on until you have mastered it in the shed.

With the brushes, you should break down where the challenges are, keeping in mind the sound that is in your head and trying to be intentional about focusing your work in those targeted areas. Be honest with yourself: if you don't hear what you are truly looking for, then keep practicing until you do.

Time Management While Practicing

Time management while practicing should be one of your key priorities. I meet drummers and students all the time who are feeling challenged with their brushes or on the kit in general, and I often ask them, "Are you practicing?" They tell me that they are practicing, but when I ask about how they are practicing and the amount of time they are dedicating to working on a specific issue that's frustrating them, then I get the real answer. Usually, it's either not nearly enough time focusing on the challenge or it's time spent too haphazardly to be a truly productive practice. You can practice brushes for one minute or five hours a day, but if your practice time isn't goal-oriented, intentional, and self-critical of your technique, then that time is wasted.

Practice Schedule Template

If I have 60 minutes:

- 10 minutes on select rudiments using the metronome with snares off
- 10 minutes on select rudiments using the metronome with snares off and adding my bass drum and hi-hat to the mix on all four quarter notes
- 10 minutes on select rudiments using the metronome with snares off and adding the ride cymbal with hi-hat and bass drum
- 10 minutes of trading fours and eights with myself
- 10 minutes of playing the brushes
- 10 minutes of playing with a record or a couple of tunes

This is what works for me. Restrictions in time and practice space may mean something different for you, but just remember the importance of spending whatever time you have to practice by practicing right.

Practice for Personal Satisfaction, Glory, or Gigs

As far back as I can remember, I always wanted to play the drums and tour around the world. I am still a chronic day-dreamer, but as a kid, it was really bad. I would be in class, and as the teacher would be explaining something, I would be envisioning myself in other faraway countries being on stage. As a young boy in Jacksonville, Florida, I didn't have a vocabulary for what that meant or even looked like, but I knew I was meant to do something beyond being in that boring class room.

My dreams evolved alongside my understanding. As a kid, I just wanted to play the drums as much as possible. Later in my teens, I knew I didn't want a regular job; I wanted a job on the drums. Once I heard Lewis Nash, I knew I wanted to move to New York. At the heart of it all, my dream is still the same in many ways as my younger self who didn't even know what he was praying for exactly: to be an in-demand jazz musician playing stages around the world.

But when I reflect on my initial years of practicing, I didn't have the stages of the world in my head. I had one goal, and that was simply to get better and play up to the high standards I had set for myself and those that, by example, my musical mentors and idols were constantly encouraging me to reach. Back then, I wasn't concerned about gig opportunities or what might be considered superficial personal gains–I just wanted to be better. I wanted my brushes to sound like Ricky Kirkland or Lewis Nash; that was it.

Most of the great musicians who have accomplished a high level of mastery have done so not to earn a buck but to feed a basic desire to get better for themselves and to sound like the masters that they artistically idolize. We must keep our motives pure musically. Otherwise, I feel our growth will be stunted, and we won't fully maximize the practice time allotted.

There will be enough time in your career to focus on the kind of opportunities you want to attain, but right now, get those brushes out, practice, and commit yourself to getting better daily.

CHAPTER 22: The Sound of Jazz

In the introduction, I spoke about my first interaction with John Riley at 16 years old. One of the most impactful things he said to me was, "You sound good, but if you want to be a jazz drummer, you need to listen to Philly Joe Jones." That suggestion set a high barometer for me, and it gave me a direction and sound to reach for when playing jazz.

That guidance connected me with the masters of jazz as both a style of music and an art form. I could use their legacy of sound and tradition as a benchmark to guide me. I recommend to any student to utilize Google to look up tracks and clips from all the masters mentioned here, along with other performances of selections from the Great American Songbook. This will help you to have proper understanding of what the right sound is. Use your computer as a tool to do the research on everything that is truly a passion for you, because clearly you can now see, as Jackie McLean once said, that "all new music is behind us."

What Is the Sound of the Brushes?

When you get your first pair of brushes, it's not enough to just sit down and start having fun with them, even though that is your long-term goal. First, you have to get the sound in your ear, no matter how skilled of a musician you are otherwise. Listen to the tracks discussed in this book in addition to as many others as you can find to hear what the brushes sound like when they are at their best. It is only after doing this that you will be able to sit down at the drums with a truly deeper understanding and context for what the sound is that you are going to create.

Get the Sound in Your Ear

I remember the great bassist Ben Wolfe telling me years ago that it's easy for kids to learn how to play a funk groove because the sound is in the air all the time on the radio, Internet, and in most popular music. But the sound of jazz is not in the air anymore, and it's definitely not a part of popular music. If you want to get better at jazz, then you have to work to get the sound of the music in your ear. This is done through listening to recordings and playing with master musicians who have studied this music for years.

I went home and threw out all of my R&B and hip-hop records (I don't suggest this to anyone; I was extreme), and I committed about 10–12 years of my life to listening to only jazz records so that I could get the sound in my ear. Sure enough, it became etched into my musical memory, and I now reach for that sound every time I play the kit.

When I play music, particularly the brushes, I want the listener to feel that glorious legacy of jazz players and trace my movements back to those early jazz forefathers from a hundred years ago. There is no greater honor for me than to have an audience member or student tell me that they can hear the influences of other great drummers in my sound.

PART 7: My Voice

CHAPTER 23: My Sound

One of the great influences on my sound may surprise you: tap dancing. I was first exposed to tap dancing as a kid by the great movie *Tap* that my parents rented for my sister and me. This movie is a classic drama about the lives of some of the great tap dancers, and the cast includes Sammy Davis Jr., Gregory Hines, a young Savion Glover, Harold Nicholas, and so many other extraordinary tap dancers. That movie really stuck with me, and when I first started playing with the brushes, I realized that there is a very deep correlation between the art forms of jazz brushes and tap dancing.

Many of the great classic jazz drummers spent many years performing at variety clubs that showcased multiple types of acts within the same night. Many of the great drummers were not only friends with tap dancers but were also tap dancers themselves. Buddy Rich was a decent tap dancer, and the legendary Sammy Davis Jr. was a great drummer. You can find multiple videos of Sammy singing, dancing, and playing the drums with a big band on YouTube.

To talk about the foundation of my sound is to mention again all those past musical masters we've covered in the book who gave me my artistic foundation and vocabulary, creating new synapses in my brain as I mimicked their skill and nuances. My sound would not exist without their sound; yet like all things, sound evolves, so my sound is reflective of the jazz legacy that is also unique to me.

Case in point: a few years ago, I was doing a jazz cruise with the Christian McBride Trio. There were many esteemed drummers on this cruise, and one of my favorite brush players, Jeff Hamilton, came to our show. I was shaking in my boots! There are only a handful of drummers that make me truly nervous when they are in the room when I'm playing, and Jeff is one of them.

We played our set which included a feature piece, "Easy Walker," written by Dr. Billy Taylor. This song literally features the brushes. Checking my breathing and calming myself internally, I just listened to the cats, made music with them, and we all had fun. At the end of the gig, Hamilton came up to me and said, "Ulysses, you're really unique, and you got this obsession with single strokes—that's pretty special." I laughed and couldn't say anything more than, "Man, I am just honored to have you in the room!"

But later, I thought about what exactly he'd said, and that night—really for the first time—I understood that I was starting to successfully build my own vocabulary on the kit… and with the brushes particularly. It really brought home to me that my near 10,000 hours of practice were paying off, because I could truly trust my own instincts and ideas. I have spent most of my life doing the work: the practicing, listening, and watching. The patience that all of that took was a lot, but the payoff was worth it. I started to have a special confidence knowing that, through all that others had taught me, I could really have some fun.

How Do You Find Your Own Sound?

One of the questions that I get so often about my playing is about finding my sound and what gave me an individual approach to the drumset. To be honest, I never sought out to have my own thing. I spent a lot of time trying to imitate my teachers like Lewis Nash. I remember bugging Nash about some technical things he was doing at some point, and he said, "Ulysses, you can be a much better 'you' than 'me.' Work on that." Those are words to live by. Don't try to be somebody else, but at the same time, don't set out to be overly focused on what makes your sound your own until you have practiced enough to start creating your own musical vocabulary on the kit.

In the next chapter, I will give you a few concepts, techniques, and exercises that are signature to my sound for those that want to discover more…

CHAPTER 24: Articulation

I found a great video online of Jimmy Slyde, another great tap legend, along with Papa Jo Jones and George Benson, and the interplay between Slyde and Jones is so incredible. When I think about my goals in terms of articulation and clarity on the brushes, I hear tap dancers in my head. It's a huge connection for me. I get a lot of positive feedback on articulation of the brushes, and other than the internal tapping, I help achieve that by keeping four points in focus while playing the brushes: the feel, clarity of touch, phrasing, and rudiments.

> **The Feel:** I want the sound of the brushes to feel good to me and the ensemble. Most of this book is about the traditional swing pattern, because it can take a while to get it to sound good and swinging.

Pick three tempos (80 bpm, 120 bpm, and 150 bpm) and play the traditional pattern on the snare drum while feathering the bass drum and playing the hi-hat on beats 2 and 4. Get everything sounding really good and then double the tempo. I find that working on my brush feel at varying tempos instead of just focusing on one tempo really allows my playing to be more solid.

> **Clarity of Touch:** When I play my brush ideas, I am singing them in my head. I always say, "If you can't play it, then sing it first." If you think about it, the desire for your brush playing should be the same as it is for your public speaking, and one of the characteristics of great speakers is the clarity of speech. Think about Martin Luther King Jr.; you don't have to struggle to hear and understand what he is saying. His diction is precise, and his words are intentional. I want the brushes to speak with the same clarity that other wonderful speakers achieve. Many times, just like when words tumble out of our mouths in a hasty jumble, we have a cluttered way of playing. This is because we are rushing and not playing things slowly and with clarity.

Take three difficult rudiments: paradiddle-diddle, flamadiddle, and a double-stroke roll. Play each of them really slow, to the point where it becomes annoying, and make sure each stroke is even, balanced, and played in the center of the drum.

Flamadiddle

Double Stroke Roll

Phrasing: To me, the type of phrasing and feel that sets jazz drummers and other drummers apart is the swing. The swing is certainly a key characteristic to my sound. I want the sound of bebop in everything that I play, and that's something I feel a lot of younger drummers don't focus on. With that said, you've got to hear the swing (triplet rhythm) in your sound!

Rudiments: From the time I was really young, I have had a fascination with drum rudiments. When I started listening to jazz drumming, the first influence that inspired me was Philly Joe Jones, who is one of the most dynamic players ever. I also was deeply inspired by Buddy Rich, who had great technique and heavily utilized rudiments in his playing. When I started to play and learn the brushes, particularly regarding brush solos, I became fascinated in my practice time with learning rudiments.

While playing the following rudiments, I want you to sing the triplet feel and play them with that emphasis.

Five-Stroke Roll

This is one of my favorite rudiments, and it sounds fantastic with the brushes. Make sure while playing this exercise that you focus on the tips; this way, your articulation will be clearer on the drum.

1. Play a regular five-stroke roll on the snare drum.
2. Now, turn on the metronome to 100 bpm, and feather the bass drum on beat 4 with the hi-hat on beats 2 and 4. Then, I want you to play the five-stroke roll.
3. Now, with the bass drum and hi-hat, I want you to play this roll again, but swing it this time.
4. Lastly, take the five-stroke roll, alternate your starting hands, swing it, and play the first phrase on the snare drum, high tom, floor tom, and then back to the snare drum.

Flam

I feel like this rudiment is not addressed as much amongst jazz drummers, but I have so much fun using it for drum fills and solo language. The key with this exercise is to keep the separation of hand height in mind when approaching this while playing the snare drum.

1. Play a regular flam on the snare drum.
2. Now, turn on the metronome to 100 bpm, and feather the bass drum on beat 4 with the hi-hat on beats 2 and 4. Then, I want you to play the flam.
3. Now, with the bass drum and hi-hat, I want you to play the flam again, but swing it this time.
4. Lastly, take the flam, alternate your starting hands, swing it, and play the first phrase on the snare drum, high tom, floor tom, and then back to the snare drum.

Paradiddle

Philly Joe Jones and Buddy Rich used this rudiment frequently. I think it's such a great one for playing around the kit, especially in getting your hands to sound cohesive. Use the tips of the brushes on this one so that you are clearer in your articulation.

1. Play a normal paradiddle on the snare drum.
2. Now turn on the metronome to 100 bpm, and feather the bass drum on beat 4 with the hi-hat on beats 2 and 4. Then, I want you to play the paradiddle.
3. Now with the bass drum and hi-hat, I want you to play this paradiddle again, but swing it while still accenting on beat 1.
4. Lastly, take the paradiddle, alternate your starting hands, swing it, and play the first phrase on the snare drum, high tom, floor tom, and then back to the snare drum.

Drag

I have always loved this rudiment because it's great for intros into solos or tunes, and it's a hip way to play nice, subtle fills with the brushes. When you play the drag with brushes, it can truly make the left hand stronger. This is something you want particularly, because when playing brushes, the left hand gets used to only "sweeping." Using this rudiment wakes the left hand up and gets it more involved in the rhythmic conversation.

1. Play a normal drag on the snare drum.
2. Now, turn on the metronome to 100 bpm, and feather the bass drum on beat 4 with the hi-hat on beats 2 and 4. Then, I want you to play the drag.
3. Now, with the bass drum and hi-hat, I want you to play this drag again, but swing it while still accenting on beat 1.
4. Lastly, take the drag, alternate your starting hands, swing it, and play the first phrase on the snare drum, high tom, floor tom, and then back to the snare drum.

CHAPTER 25: How to Craft a Drum Solo

"Ulysses, How Do You Approach Soloing?"

This is probably the most-asked question I receive around the world when I teach and interact with young drummers. My response to them, as you might have guessed by now is, "You shouldn't be concerned about soloing; play time."

Now, this statement is unfair because soloing is a true art form. It's not spoken about often as it pertains to the brushes, but keeping time is the root from which my soloing grows. By now, you already know the sanctity in which I hold good time-keeping. We have explored a number of rudiments and exercises to help strengthen your articulation and clarity of sound, which is also crucial for soloing. In my mind, there are two other important components to soloing: vocabulary and learning the musical form of the tune.

Vocabulary

For any person that has ever tried to learn a new language in school, you know that you spend many years mastering phrases and words that are utilized within that language. If you continue studying, then at some point, you will need to actually speak to someone to get all of that study formulated into a conversation.

What does this mean for drummers? The answer is that, basically, you have to get musical vocabulary into your hands.

Most of the young drummers I have worked with ask how they can have more ideas for soloing. Ultimately, it's just like if you want to write a book: first you know a wide vocabulary of words, then you put them together in different ways until the vocabulary says what you want. But, it first comes down to getting that musical vocabulary into your hands. You can't write a book if you only know 10 words, and you can't create a memorable solo if your vocabulary is too limited to manifest what you want to say.

Questions About Vocabulary

I have offered some questions below, and I believe if you take the time to answer them, they will help lead you to multiple extra-curricular assignments, and ultimately to a method that will allow you to build your vocabulary rapidly.

1. Have you transcribed any brush solos?
2. Have you transcribed a solo from Kenny Clarke?
3. Have you transcribed a solo from Vernel Fournier?
4. Have you listened to a recording of Papa Jo Jones or Zutty Singleton and tried to imitate their phrasing?

Assignment: Do the work so that all of the answers to the questions above become a *yes*. For the younger players, you can just transcribe a phrase from one of the masters and work on incorporating that into your playing.

Learn the Musical Form of the Tune

It's impossible to be a great soloist if you don't know the tune you're going to solo on. Like with any other solo, when you're playing with brushes, you want to have an innate understanding of the kinds of possibilities the song is providing to you. After all, a solo is a riff and expression on the song being played, not just a drummer randomly expressing themselves. If you don't know the song, then that may be part of the reason why you may be struggling with soloing. This is because you don't truly understand what you are soloing on.

Traditional song forms for jazz revolve around many different harmonic cycles, and I'll talk about two below. This is usually very difficult for drummers if they don't have knowledge or a connection to the piano or a chordal instrument like the guitar. I encourage all of you to use this as an opportunity to form a deeper relationship with these chordal instruments so that your understanding of harmony can be broadened and make you a better musician.

Blues Form: This musical form is based typically on a 12-bar form with a basic I–IV–V harmonic progression.

Rhythm Changes: This form is based on a 32-bar structure and is played often in the jazz format on songs like "Oleo," "Anthropology," and many others.

You want to be able to hear the top, middle, and the end of the form. Being able to mark that in playing time can really make you a rare drummer that musicians love to play with. You can also learn in the beginning of your development to count 12, 16, or 24 bars to keep yourself focused during the form. Make sure you pay attention and count while listening to some of the play-along tracks provided with this book.

CHAPTER 26: Key Points to Help with Soloing

Here's a step-by-step process that you can use to aid your soloing on the brushes:

1. Learn to sing the melody of *every tune* (e.g., the blues standard "Now's the Time").
2. Now, sing the harmonic progression (e.g., blues form for one chorus).
3. Sing the melody and hear the blues form in your mind while playing swing time for one chorus.
4. At this point, you should be able to hear the melody, harmonic form, and solo for one chorus.

How did that turn out for you?

Keep repeating this exercise until you get comfortable and feel like you are making music. You can extend the choruses as well. Once you can play well over a blues form, work on other musical jazz forms.

Snare Drum

With the brushes, a key element in soloing for me was firstly learning how to play the snare drum to get various ideas flowing from that drum only. As a brush player, there are so many playing points that you can use when you focus on the snare.

I remember watching Herlin Riley play at a show one night in New Orleans, and during his performance he played with *everything* on the drumset—the rims, the side of the drums, even the pipes that were part of the wall on stage! That taught me something really profound: as drummers, we are gifted with so many accessories that are actually part of the kit and snare drum, so let's use them! I think it's fantastic to explore these possibilities, and you can become a better soloist when you maximize each instrument and let your musical imagination run wild.

Herlin Riley

Around the Kit

Young drummers who are used to playing other genres of music will often wonder why, in jazz, we only play a four-piece kit. I say that's more than enough drums for me to make music with. As a brush player, once you really learn how to maximize your vocabulary on the snare drum, you can then begin to move around the kit to the toms and cymbals. You'll find a whole new world of sound. Most young drummers are afraid to move around the kit, but I want to challenge you.

Exercise

Take one rudiment or a phrase, and play it on the snare drum, high tom, floor tom, and then back to the snare drum. Do this in time while playing the hi-hat and feathering the bass drum. This will allow you to open up on the kit and explore beyond the normal patterns and methods you are accustomed to using while soloing.

Learn How to Tell a Story

All great stories have a beginning, middle, and end. It's hard to know exactly what a beginning, middle, and end look like in a story that isn't 300 pages and instead resembles something more concise and personal, like a song. If you aren't sure, then there is a great podcast called *The Moth* where you can listen to short, poignant stories from all walks of life. I always say to drummers in my studio, "If you want to learn how to be a great soloist, then you need to learn how to tell a story." What story do you hear yourself telling when you solo?

Example

Beginning: Take a phrase that basically says, "Hello. I am [state your name], and I am here to say this..." Make your musical statement on the drums, and make sure it's a true entrance, not only in volume, but also in approach and style.

Middle: Now that you have introduced yourself, what is going to be the "plot" or the substance of the story? Take the listener on a journey, getting them fully engaged with your sound, message, and ideas.

End: It's time now to bring this solo to a climactic closing point. Growing up in the Pentecostal church, the end of the sermon was always the most exciting part because when you had a great preacher, they knew how to bring their sermon "home." This would leave the people with an understanding of the focal point of what the preacher wanted to say.

Like the great preachers and jazz masters I learned from, when I end a solo, I sometimes touch back to the initial idea or melody within the tune.

PART 8: The Conclusion

CHAPTER 27: How Do I Approach This Music?

"Mr. Taste"

There is a great man and unsurpassed fan of jazz drumming I know in New York named Sal Capozucca. Many years ago, he anointed me with the nick-name "Mr. Taste." I didn't understand entirely what he meant until I started getting more comfortable with my own sound and feeling confident about what is valuable about my playing–not just to others, but also to myself. One of my joys musically is being able to accent the subtle nuances in the music, and I can especially do this with the brushes. To me, they are the superior way to really mirror the sound and textures of other instruments.

No matter your level at the kit, learn to value your sound now and appreciate the progress. None of us should ever stop practicing and learning, and even with all of that, none of us may ever reach true perfection in our art. However, we can be proud of ourselves every step of the way as long as we're working hard to be at our personal best. To me, "Mr. Taste" means adhering to a philosophy that the music matters most. So when I want to play a brush fill, add an accent, or solo, I want to make sure that I express myself... but with class.

One of the classiest accessories a drummer has is space. To me, it is one of the greatest tools in music. Space is such a great device to use, and when you use it right, it is always so tasteful. For me, that is my goal whenever I play brushes. I want the audience to go on a beautiful journey with me as musician, and I guide that journey as carefully and tastefully as I can.

Take all of your musical ideas and apply space. My guess is you'll find some "tastiness" make its way into your playing as well. Above all, make sure you're playing for the music.

Have Fun with the Brushes

Music is something that has always been my release and escape throughout much of my life. I have been playing the drums since I was two years of age, and the only way you can maintain a relationship with something that long is to constantly figure out new ways to have fun with it.

Drummer vs. Musician

I always ask my students:

- What kind of drummer are you?
- What kind of musician are you?
- What are your strengths and weaknesses as a drummer?
- What are your strengths and weaknesses as a musician?

Staying in tune with your answers to these questions will allow you not only to improve your solos with brushes and sticks, but it will positively affect your approach to music and life.

"All New Music Is Behind Us"—Jackie McLean

We have visited this theme numerous times, so you can see how important I believe this concept to be: you need to look to the past, to those greater than you whom you admire. If you don't see all that has been done before you, then what will make you want to be better than where you currently are? After that monumental day when Ricky Kirkland first introduced the sound of the brushes to me, I went on a musical escapade of listening to all the great brush players throughout time that I could find tracks for. That journey truly changed my life. Hearing what these guys did in their approach to the brushes absolutely defined the kind of player I wanted to become. I am giving you a list of my favorite drummers who play brushes, along with listening examples of their playing for you to enjoy and learn from.

It is so important to study the masters constantly because there is not one teacher, book, nor even the greatest talent that can make you truly understand the fundamental basics of the brushes. Without that, where are you? You have to listen to find your own drumming "North Star" to guide your personal journey on the brushes, and how to play them to the fullest.

Benny Golson once told me: "You practice so that you can alleviate the instrument as an obstacle in expression in the heat of the moment."

This is a tool; learn from it and don't forget to *have fun*!

Keep swingin'!

U

Index of Recordings

In this section, I have compiled a playlist of recordings that have been incredibly formative for me in my own learning process, playing, and musical development. I am certain there are recordings that may not be on this list that people otherwise feel should be included. To those people I apologize. We are lucky enough to have so very many recordings from the past and present right here in our grasp, and we have the luxury to argue about which of them are, nuance by nuance, better than the rest. My first goal with this playlist was to represent players that are part of the early jazz tradition in line with the evolution of the sound and technique of the brushes. Second, I wanted to include players that are often listed as accomplished drummers with great brush technique and who have made a huge impact on my playing through the years.

I thought the best way to sort these tracks is in order of the technological evolution of the brushes as it aligns with the development of jazz. You can search via YouTube, Apple Music, Spotify, or other platforms.

My desire as someone who has studied the jazz brushes for many years would be for every drummer to check out all of these amazing tracks. You can listen to the whole list or just parts of it. I wanted to give you a fair breadth of recorded examples to have as a reference in order to improve not only your playing, but also your knowledge about the great brush players out there.

Early Jazz Drummers

Andrew Hilaire
Artist: Jelly Roll Morton's Red Hot Peppers
Song: "Grandpa's Spells" (1926)

Harry Dial
Artist: Harry Dial's Bluesicians
Song: "Poison" (1930)

Artist: Alex Hill & His Orchestra
Song: "Dyin' with the Blues" (1930)

Kaiser Marshall
Artist: McKinney's Cotton Pickers
Song: "Miss Hannah" (1929)
Song: "Wherever There's a Will, There's a Way" (1929)

Johnny Wells
Artist: Jimmie Noone's Apex Club Orchestra
Song: "Monday Date" (1928)

Artist: Alex Hill
Song: "Stompin' 'Em Down" (1929)

Stan King
Artist: The Dorsey Brothers
Song: "Breakaway" (1929)

Tommy Benford
Artist: Jelly Roll Morton's Red Hot Peppers
Song: "Mournful Serenade" (1928)
Song: "Shreveport Stomp" (1928)

Walter Bishop
Artist: Dixie Rhythm Kings
Song: "Story Book Ball" (1930)

Walter Johnson
Artist: Fletcher Henderson
Song: "You Rascal You" (1931)

Warren "Baby" Dodds
Artist: Jelly Roll Morton Trio
Song: "Mr. Jelly Lord" (1927)
Song: "Wolverine Blues" (1927)

Artist: Jelly Roll Morton's Red Hot Peppers
Song: "Beale Street Blues" (1927)

Zutty Singleton
Artist: Jelly Roll Morton
Song: "Smilin' the Blues Away" (1929)

Artist: Louis Armstrong and His Orchestra
Song: "Muggles" (1929)

Swing & Bebop Drummers

Art Blakey
Artist: Cannonball Adderley
Album: Somethin' Else (1958)
Song: "Love for Sale"

Artist: Lee Morgan
Album: Here's Lee Morgan (1960)
Song: "I'm a Fool to Want You"

Art Taylor
Artist: Red Garland
Album: A Garland of Red (1957)
Song: "A Foggy Day"
Song: "What Is This Thing Called Love?"

Buddy Rich
Artist: Ella Fitzgerald and Louis Armstrong
Album: Ella and Louis (1956)
Song: "Can't We Be Friends?"
Song: "Isn't This a Lovely Day?"

Artist: Art Tatum Trio
Album: Best of Art Tatum (1987)
Song: "Hallelujah"

Ed Thigpen
Artist: Oscar Peterson Trio
Album: We Get Requests (1964)
Song: "The Days of Wine and Roses"
Song: "Have You Met Miss Jones?"

Eddie Locke
Artist: Warren Vaché
Album: What Is There to Say? (2000)
Song: "Too Phat Blues"

Artist: Warren Vaché
Album: Dream Dancing (2004)
Song: "Too Late Now"

YouTube keywords:
"Eddie Locke, The Art of Playing Brushes"
Song: "3/4 Time"

Gene Krupa
Artist: Gene Krupa & His Orchestra
Song: "Wire Brush Stomp" (1938)

Jack DeJohnette
Artist: Keith Jarrett
Album: Tokyo '96 (1998)
Song: "It Could Happen to You"
Song: "Summer Night"

Jake Hanna
Artist: Jake Hanna
Abum: The Joint Is Jumpin' (1998)
Song: "Exactly Like You"
Song: "My Ideal"

Jimmy Cobb
Artist: Miles Davis
Album: Kind of Blue (1959)
Song: "Blue in Green"

Kenny Clarke
Artist: Lee Konitz with Warne Marsh
Album: Lee Konitz with Warne Marsh (1955)
Song: "Two Not One"

Artist: Hank Jones
Album: Bluebird (1956)
Song: "Wine and Brandy"
Song: "Alpha"

Louis Bellson
Artist: Count Basie and Oscar Peterson
Album: Satch and Josh... Again (1977)
Song: "Roots"
Song: "Sweethearts on Parade"

O'Neil Spencer
Artist: John Kirby Sextet
Song: "Front and Center" (1939)
Song: "It Feels So Good" (1939)
Song: "Royal Garden Blues" (1939)

"Papa" Jo Jones
Artist: Kansas City Five
Song: "I Know That You Know" (1938)

Artist: Jo Jones
Album: The Essential Jo Jones (1977)
Song: "Satin Doll"
*Song: "Sweet Georgia Brown"

*He starts out with his hands, and then plays brushes for the instrumental solos, and his drum solo is with his hands.

"Philly" Joe Jones
Artist: Miles Davis
Album: Milestones (1958)
Song: "Billy Boy"

Artist: Wynton Kelly
Album: Kelly at Midnight (1960)
Song: "Temperance"

Artist: Philly Joe Jones
Album: Mo' Joe (1968)
Song: "Here's That Rainy Day"

Roy Haynes
Artist: Sarah Vaughan
Album: At Mister Kelly's (1957)
Song: "How High the Moon"

Artist: Roy Haynes Quartet
Album: Out of the Afternoon (1962)
Song: "Some Other Spring"

Artist: Chick Corea
Album: Now He Sings, Now He Sobs (1968)
Song: "My One and Only Love"

Sid Catlett
Artist: Big Sid Catlett Quartet ft. Ben Webster
Song: "Just a Riff" (1944)

Post Bebop Drummers

Adonis Rose
Artist: Nicholas Payton
Album: Gumbo Nouveau (1995)
Song: "I Gotta Right to Sing the Blues"

Artist: Adonis Rose
Album: On the Verge (2007)
Song: "Lies in Beauty"

Alan Dawson
YouTube keywords:
"Alan Dawson, Rudimental Rituals"

Ali Jackson
Artist: Wynton Marsalis Quartet
Album: The Magic Hour (2004)
Song: "Sophie Rosa Lee"

Artist: Ali Jackson
Album: Amalgamations (2014)
Song: "Ali Got Rhythm"

Ari Hoenig
Artist: Ari Hoenig Trio
Album: Conner's Days (2019)
Song: "Prelude to a Kiss"

Antonio Sánchez
Artist: Antonio Sánchez
Album: Three Times Three (2014)
Song: "Big Dream"

Bill Stewart
Artist: Bill Stewart
Album: Band Menu (2018)
Song: "Re: Person I Knew"

Artist: Larry Goldings, Peter Bernstein, Bill Stewart
Album: Toy Tunes (2018)
Song: "I'm in the Mood for Love"

Billy Drummond
Artist: Billy Drummond
Album: Native Colours (1994)
Track: "One for Walton"

Artist: David Hazeltine-George Mraz Trio
Album: Manhattan (2006)
Track: "In Your Own Sweet Way"

Billy Higgins
Artist: VIP Trio
Album: Standards (1988)
Song: "Easy Walker"
Song: "It Might as Well Be Spring"

Brian Blade
Artist: Kenny Garrett
Album: Triology (1995)
Song: "A Time for Love"

Artist: Sam Yahel Trio
Album: Trio (1999)
Song: "Blues for Bulgaria"

Carl Allen
Artist: Carl Allen and Manhattan Projects
Album: Piccadilly Square (1989)
Song: "Lullaby of Birdland"

Artist: Christian McBride & Inside Straight
Album: Kind of Brown (2009)
Song: "Uncle James"

Clarence Penn
Artist: Cyrus Chestnut
Album: Revelation (1994)
Song: "Blues for Nita"
Song: "Little Ditty"

Damion Reid
Artist: Matt Brewer
Album: Ganymede (2019)
Song: "Ganymede"
Song: "When Sunny Gets Blue"

Donald Edwards
Artist: Dayna Stephens
Album: Today Is Tomorrow (2012)
Song: "Haden's Largo"

Artist: Ben Wolfe
Album: From Here I See (2013)
Song: "Baby Tiger"

Elvin Jones
Artist: Tommy Flanagan
Album: Eclypso (1980)
Song: "Oleo"
Song: "A Blue Time"

Eric Harland
Artist: Jimmy Greene
Album: Gifts and Givers (2007)
Song: "Greene Blues"

Artist: Joel Weiskopf
Album: Devoted to You (2007)
Song: "Giving Thanks"

Greg Hutchinson
Artist: Ray Brown
Album: Live at Scullers (1996)
Song: "Bye Bye Blackbird"
Song: "But Not for Me"

Herlin Riley
Artist: Wynton Marsalis
Album: Standard Time Vol. 3: The Resolution of Romance (1990)
Songs: "Bona and Paul"
Song: "A Sleepin' Bee"

Artist: Wynton and Ellis Marsalis
Album: Joe Cool's Blues (1995)
Song: "On Peanuts Playground"

Artist: Cécile McLorin Salvant
Album: WomanChild (2013)
Song: "WomanChild"

Jamison Ross
Artist: Jamison Ross
Album: Jamison (2015)
Song: "Epiphany"

Artist: Jamison Ross
Album: All for One (2018)
Song: "Everybody's Cryin' Mercy"

Jason Brown
Artist: Joey DeFrancesco
Album: Project Freedom (2017)
Song: "Peace Bridge"

Jeff Hamilton
Artist: Akiko Tsuruga
Album: So Cute, So Bad (2017)
Song: "Frame for the Blues"

Artist: Jeff Hamilton Trio
Album: Red Sparkle (2012)
Song: "Bye Ya"
Song: "Too Marvelous for Words"

Jeff "Tain" Watts
Artist: Wynton Marsalis
Album: Marsalis Standard Time Vol. 1 (1987)
Song: "Cherokee"
Song: "New Orleans"

Artist: Harry Connick Jr.
Album: When Harry Met Sally… (1989)
Song: "It Had to Be You"

Jeremy "Bean" Clemmons
Artist: Sullivan Fortner
Album: Moments Preserved (2018)
Song: "Elegy for Clyde Kerr, Jr."
Song: "Eyes So Beautiful as Yours"

John Hollenbeck
Artist: John Hollenbeck
Album: Songs I Like a Lot (2013)
Song: "Wichita Lineman"

Joe Morello
Artist: Joe Morello
Album: It's About Time (1962)
Song: "Ev'ry Time"
Song: "Time After Time"

Joe Farnsworth
Artist: Wynton Marsalis
Album: Live at the House of Tribes (2005)
Song: "Just Friends"
Song: "What Is This Thing Called Love?"

Joey Baron
Artist: John Abercrombie
Album: Cat 'n' Mouse (2002)
Song: "A Nice Idea"

Johnathan Blake
Artist: Black Art Jazz Collective
Album: Armor of Pride (2018)
Song: "Awuraa Amma"

Artist: Johnathan Blake
Album: Trion (2019)
Song: "Trope"

Jonathan Barber
Artist: Jonathan Barber
Album: Vision Ahead (2018)
Song: "Think On These Things"

Karriem Riggins
Artist: Carmen McRae
Album: At the Great American Music Hall (1977)
Song: "Them There Eyes"

Artist: Ray Brown
Album: Live at Starbucks (2001)
Song: "Our Delight"
Song: "When I Fall in Love"

Kendrick Scott
Artist: Gretchen Parlato
Album: In a Dream (2009)
Song: "Within Me"

Artist: Kendrick Scott
Album: Reverence (2009)
Song: "Metamorphosis"

Kenny Washington
Artist: Bill Charlap
Album: All Through the Night (1998)
Song: "All Through the Night"

Artist: Bill Charlap
Album: Stardust (2002)
Song: "I Walk with Music"

Kyle Poole
Artist: Emmet Cohen Trio
Album: Dirty in Detroit (2018)
Song: "You Don't Know What Love Is"

Lawrence Leathers
Artist: Cécile McLorin Salvant
Album: For One to Love (2015)
Song: "Growlin' Dan"
Song: "Stepsisters' Lament"

Lenny White
Artist: Chaka Khan, Chick Corea, Joe Henderson, Freddie Hubbard, Stanley Clarke, Lenny White
Album: Echoes of an Era (1982)
Song: "I Hear Music"
Song: "All of Me"

Lewis Nash
Artist: Lewis Nash
Album: Rhythm Is My Business (1989)
Song: "My Shining Hour"

Artist: Tommy Flanagan
Album: Lady Be Good… For Ella (1994)
Song: "Love You Madly"

Marcus Baylor
Artist: Jean Baylor
Album: Light Up the World (2011)
Song: "You Are (The Greatest Gift)"

Marcus Gilmore
Artist: Danny Grissett
Album: Stride (2011)
Song: "Two Sleepy People"

Artist: Lage Lund Four
Album: Live at Smalls (2012)
Song: "Soliloquy"

Matt Wilson
Artist: Matt Wilson Quartet
Album: Smile (1999)
Song: "Strangers in the Night"

Mel Lewis
Artist: Herbie Mann
Album: The Herbie Mann String Album (1967)
Song: "Sports Car"

Artist: Thad Jones & Mel Lewis
Album: Live at the Village Vanguard (1967)
Song: "The Little Pixie"

Artist: Thad Jones & Mel Lewis
Album: Consummation (1970)
Song: "Tiptoe"

Milt Turner
Artist: Hank Crawford
Album: The Soul Clinic (1962)
Song: "What a Difference a Day Makes"

Montez Coleman
Artist: Gerald Cannon
Album: Gerald Cannon (2003)
Song: "Faith"

Artist: Roy Hargrove
Album: Earfood (2008)
Song: "Joy Is Sorrow Unmasked"

Nasheet Waits
Artist: Christian McBride
Album: Christian McBride's New Jawn (2018)
Song: "Ballad of Ernie Washington"

Neal Smith
Artist: Cyrus Chestnut
Album: You Are My Sunshine (2003)
Song: "God Has Smiled On Me"
Song: "Erroling"

Obed Calvaire
Artist: The Clayton Brothers
Album: Soul Brothers (2016)
Song: "Memories of Absent Time"
Song: "Saturday Night Special"

Paul Wertico
Artist: Kurt Elling
Album: This Time It's Love (1998)
Song: "I Feel So Smoochie"

Artist: Kurt Elling
Album: Man in the Air (2003)
Song: "Never My Love"

Peter Erskine
Artist: Kurt Elling
Album: Flirting with Twilight (2001)
Song: "You Don't Know What Love Is"

Quentin Baxter
Artist: René Marie
Album: Sound of Red (2016)
Song: "Colorado River Song"
Song: "If You Were Mine"

Rodney Green
Artist: Eric Reed
Album: E-Bop (2003)
Song: "Grew-vy"

Artist: Mulgrew Miller
Album: Live at the Kennedy Center, Volume One (2006)
Song: "Relaxin' at Camarillo"

Roy McCurdy
Artist: Jon Mayer
Album: Nightscape (2009)
Song: "The Touch of Your Lips"

Shannon Powell
Artist: Harry Connick, Jr.
Album: Blue Light, Red Light (1991)
Song: "If I Could Give You More"

Artist: Russell Malone
Album: Russell Malone (1992)
Song: "London by Night"

Artist: Dr. Michael White
Album: Blue Crescent (2008)
Song: "Blue Crescent"

Terreon "Tank" Gully
Artist: Stefon Harris
Album: African Tarantella (2006)
Song: "From the Gardner Meditation: African Tarantella"

Tony Reedus
Artist: Kenny Garrett
Album: Introducing Kenny Garrett (1985)
Song: "Have You Met Miss Jones?"

Artist: Benny Green Quintet
Album: Prelude (1988)
Song: "Countdown"

Vernel Fournier
Artist: Ahmad Jamal Trio
Album: At the Pershing: But Not for Me (1958)
Song: "The Surrey with the Fringe on Top"
Song: "Moonlight in Vermont

Willie Jones III
Artist: Roy Hargrove
Album: Moment to Moment (1999)
Song: "Always and Forever"

Artist: Kurt Elling
Album: Nightmoves (2007)
Song: "Tight"

Ulysses Owens Jr.
Artist: Ulysses Owens Jr.
Album: Unanimous (2012)
Song: "Cherokee"

Artist: Christian McBride Trio
Album: Out Here (2013)
Song: "East of the Sun"
Song: "Easy Walker"

Artist: Kurt Elling and James Morrison
Album: Live in New York (2019)
Song: "Benny's from Heaven"
Song: "Brother Where Are You"

Tap Dancers

Tap dancing is one of the most powerful art forms to me. As a drummer and brush player, I think there is so much that we can learn from great tap dancers from the past and present. Here is a list of some great tap dancers that have influenced me and who I think you should check out.

Old School

Bunny Briggs

Chuck Green

Jimmy Slyde

Gregory Hines

Maurice Hines

Nicholas Brothers

Savion Glover

Sammy Davis Jr.

Sandman Sims

New Generation

Brinae Ali

DeWitt Fleming Jr.

Jason Samuels Smith

Joseph Wiggan

Michela Lerman

Michelle Dorrance

There is actually a great tribute video to Sammy Davis Jr. with many of these dancers on the same stage. My sister Iris showed me this clip and I was mesmerized. Just go to YouTube, type in the keywords "Nicholas Brothers, Sammy Davis Jr. tribute," and you should be able to find the video.

Acknowledgments

I am grateful to the creative ideas and thoughts that all derive from God and for the gifts and awareness of them at this moment in time.

Mom and Dad: thank you for always believing in me and supporting me 120 percent in every dream I have. Iris and Felicia: thanks for being my constant cheerleaders. Thanks to the Don't Miss a Beat staff and families for supporting me through this process. Also, thanks to Michael Yanover, Alexander Smalls, Rickey Minor, Randy Hall, and Steve Jordan, who are my mentors and are often challenging me to be better.

Thanks to my friends who have always encouraged me to write and be my best self: LaFredrick Coaxner, Tonya Bell, Alicia Olatuja, Kalyn Dean, Sterling Cummings, Tawan Davis, Chloe Davis, Adam Burton, Tim Green, Michael Dease, and Stephen Duhart.

Unlimited Myles Management: Myles, Lorraine, and Rory. Thanks for keeping me focused and always believing in me.

Shola Adisa Ferrar for giving me courage to write. To Arlen Gargagliano and Geveryl Robinson: you are so integral to what I do as a writer and author. Charles Burchell: thanks for your encouragement and belief in my writing voice.

Matthew Rybicki: I appreciate you for hearing my idea and leading me to Eric Wills and Jeff Schroedl, which got this project started. To the Hal Leonard team (Eric, Jeff, Jen, Steve, Bonnie, and Nancy): thank you for being so gracious and supportive to me during this process. Derek you are the man and you truly brought this project to and over the finish line. Thank You.

Zack Olsen and India: I appreciate your support and love. Taylor Reinhold: thanks for visually creating what's in my head; it will help many others understand this art form. Chris Horoschak: you are the graphic and visual part of my mind, and thank you for being committed to all of my endeavors. Anna: thanks for being you and for your wonderful work. Dave Darlington, you are the mixing and mastering engineer in my life. Thanks for teaching me how to make great music.

Megan Rickman: thanks for editing my words beautifully and showing me a whole new side to my writing.

Mike, Karlea, and Matthew: thanks to each you for playing your butts off on this project, and Aaron Jennings, thanks for being part of this. Chris Sulit: thanks for documenting everything I record perfectly.

Thanks to Tim Buell and Zach Adelman for their transcribing work.

To those that gave me their time for interviews: I am so thankful and enlightened because of the time we shared. Joe Calato, Regal Tip, and the Calato family (Michelle and Matt), thanks so much. Loren Schoenberg: I appreciate you squeezing me into your busy schedule. Thanks to Eric Reed for helping me to find some records for this playlist.

Thank you to all of my drum instructors on my journey of music: Ricky Kirkland, Lewis Nash, Carl Allen, Herlin Riley, Billy Drummond, Kenny Washington, Leon Anderson, John Garren, and Brent Smedley.

Thanks to Utah State University Caine College of Arts and Dr. Jason Nicholson.

Thanks to Wynton Marsalis, Dr. Aaron Flagg, and the Juilliard School for your wisdom and guidance.

Thanks to Felix, the owner of Harlem Cigar Room and the team who were very patient and never interrupted me when I spent hours there writing this book.

Thank you to the countless masters of this art form of the brushes that would make this list too long to print.

This book is dedicated to the memory of one of the most talented time-keepers of my generation who played brushes beautifully: Lawrence Leathers. Gone too soon...

Lastly, thanks to each and every one of you that will purchase this book around the world. I hope it is a constant resource and tool of inspiration for you.

U

Musicians

It's very important to me to be intentional and aware of the musicians I choose to make music with, and the same should be true for you.

For the play-along recordings, I assembled a dynamic group of top-rate New York City-based jazz musicians for you to play and practice with consistently.

Karlea Lynné — vocalist

Karlea can be found serving music for the soul throughout the region at many venues including Minton's Playhouse, SOB's, the Cell, the House of Blues, Gin Fizz, South Jazz Kitchen, Fat Cat, the Rainbow Room, Smalls Jazz Club, and Jazz at Lincoln Center. Heavily influenced by Nancy Wilson, Sarah Vaughan, and Dinah Washington, Karlea's sound is just one of her unforgettable assets that charms every audience she encounters.

Matthew Rybicki — bassist

Raised in Cleveland, Ohio, Matthew Rybicki has performed with Wynton Marsalis and the Jazz at Lincoln Center Orchestra, Ernie Watts, Laurence Hobgood, Hilary Kole, Wycliffe Gordon, Ted Rosenthal, Mark Gould, Nnenna Freelon, Renée Fleming, Terell Stafford, Winard Harper, Mark Whitfield, Victor Goines, and Marcus Printup. He has also had the great fortune of performing at many well-respected venues in New York such as the Village Vanguard and the Blue Note, as well as concert halls and festivals in locations ranging from Italy to Qatar and Taiwan. Rybicki maintains an active performing schedule, working with his own ensembles and with many accomplished colleagues and mentors such as Lew Tabackin, Lewis Nash, Dan Nimmer, Oscar Perez, Christian Sands, Gerald Clayton, David Berger, and Charenee Wade.

Mike King — pianist

Mr. King is an alumnus of Lincoln Park High School and the prestigious Oberlin Conservatory. He was selected to attend the Thelonious Monk Institute and the Ravinia Jazz Scholars program on merit scholarships. Michael has performed with Bobby Watson, Kevin Eubanks, Dave Liebman, Gary Bartz, Billy Hart, Joel Frahm, Rufus Reid, and Antonio Hart, among others. You can currently catch Mr. King touring internationally with the Mike King Trio, Dee Dee Bridgewater, Robin Eubanks, Marquis Hill, Theo Croker, Soul Understated, Melissa Aldana, and Marcus Printup.

Contact

Please feel free to connect with me through social media and my website to tell me how this book is helping you.

Website

www.usojazzy.com

Social Media

Facebook: Ulysses Owens Jr. (Fan Page)

Instagram: @ulyssesowensjr

Twitter: @UlyssesOwensJr

Book Hashtag

#JazzBrushes4U